WINTER warmers

MORE THAN 65 COMFORTING
RECIPES FOR CHILLY DAYS

RYLAND PETERS & SMALL

Senior Designer Toni Kay
Head of Production Patricia Harrington
Creative Director Leslie Harrington
Editorial Director Julia Charles

Indexer Vanessa Bird

First published in 2025 by
Ryland Peters & Small
20–21 Jockey's Fields, London
WC1R 4BW
and
1452 Davis Bugg Road
Warrenton, NC 27589

www.rylandpeters.com
email: euregulations@rylandpeters.com

10 9 8 7 6 5 4 3 2 1

Text © Maxine Clark, Megan Davies, Liz Franklin, Dunja Gulin, Tori Haschka, Carol Hilker, Lizzie Kamanetzky, Kathy Kordalis, Jenny Linford, Theo A. Michaels, Hannah Miles, Louise Pickford, Will Torrent, Laura Washburn Hutton, Belinda Williams and Ryland Peters & Small 2025
Design and commissioned photography © Ryland Peters & Small 2025 (see full credits on page 160)

Printed in China.

The authors' moral rights have been asserted. All rights reserved. No part of this publication may be reproduced, stored in a retrieval system or transmitted in any form or by any means, electronic, mechanical, photocopying or otherwise, without the prior permission of the publisher.

ISBN: 978-1-78879-715-3

A CIP record for this book is available from the British Library.
US Library of Congress cataloging-in-Publication Data has been applied for.

The authorised representative in the EEA is Authorised Rep Compliance Ltd., Ground Floor, 71 Lower Baggot Street, Dublin, D02 P593, Ireland
www.arccompliance.com

NOTES
• All spoon measurements are level unless otherwise specified.
• All herbs used are fresh unless otherwise specified.
• All eggs are medium (UK) or large (US), unless specified as large, in which case US extra-large should be used. Uncooked or partially cooked eggs should not be served to the very old, frail, young children, pregnant women or those with compromised immune systems.
• When a recipe calls for cling film/plastic wrap, you can substitute for beeswax wraps, silicone stretch lids or compostable baking paper for greater sustainability.
• When a recipe calls for the grated zest of citrus fruit, buy unwaxed fruit and wash well before using.
• Ovens should be preheated to the specified temperatures. If using a fan-assisted oven, adjust temperatures according to the manufacturer's instructions.

Contents

Introduction 6

Hearty soups 8

Fondues & melted cheese 30

Toasties & jackets 50

Fireside snacks & suppers 72

Sweet things 108

Hot drinks 138

Index 158
Credits 160

Introduction

When the weather turns colder and the nights draw in, we all begin to crave those nourishing, hearty dishes that have the power to bring us comfort and warmth.

Indeed it's the perfect time of year to stay at home, keep warm and bring a little cosiness to meal times, from rich soups and luxurious toasties to indulgent fondues and steaming jacket potatoes topped with your favourite combinations.

The recipes in this book range from those timeless classics that will be served up with a side of nostalgia – such as Cream of Chicken Soup (see page 12), Philly Cheesesteak Sandwich (see page 57) and Baked Eggs (see page 75) – to indulgent and aromatic offerings that are traditionally enjoyed at winter markets and festive pop-ups – such as Raclette over Roasted Potatoes (see page 42), Bitter Chocolate Fondue with Churros (see page 124) and Caramel Macchiato (see page 141).

What better way is there to spend a frosty day than to invite company over for a steaming bowl of French onion soup, or perhaps a velvety cheese fondue so everyone can get involved around the table? Or why not set up a delicious fireside sharing board using a medley of ideas from this book?

The recipes here take inspiration from across the globe, but what they all have in common is the warmth and nourishment they will provide throughout the winter – a time we all need those comforting classics. With melty cheese, warming spices, steaming soups, hearty stews, indulgent sweet treats and hot beverages to sip by the fire, the following pages are sure to inspire you to savour the winter season.

HEARTY SOUPS

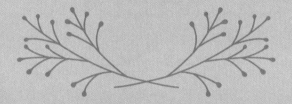

This comforting soup is a subtly spiced Indian dhal with coconut, puréed until smooth and finished with a tadka (spiced butter) for an extra-special flavour hit. It boasts myriad winter health benefits with lentils, ginger and chilli in its ingredients list. It is perfect served with naan for dipping.

Spiced lentil soup

400-ml/14-oz. can coconut milk
200 g/generous 1 cup red split lentils
1 large red chilli/chile
4 large vine tomatoes
2.5-cm/1-inch piece of ginger, peeled and finely chopped
1 teaspoon fenugreek
1 tablespoon garam masala
salt and freshly ground black pepper
2 large naan breads, sliced, to serve (optional)

FOR THE TADKA

2 tablespoons ghee or clarified butter
1 large garlic clove, thinly sliced
6 curry leaves
1 tablespoon black onion/nigella seeds

Serves 4

For the soup, heat 800 ml/3⅓ cups water and the coconut milk in a large saucepan and pour in the lentils and a pinch of salt. Cut a slit in the chilli but keep it whole as you will remove it later. Halve the tomatoes and add to the saucepan with the ginger, fenugreek and garam masala. Simmer for about 30 minutes until the lentils are soft. Remove the chilli and discard it. Transfer the soup to a blender or food processor and blitz until smooth, or use a stick blender. Return to the saucepan and season well with salt and pepper.

To prepare the tadka, heat the ghee in a small frying pan/skillet or pan, then add the garlic, curry leaves and black onion seeds and fry until the garlic just starts to turn golden brown. Take care that it does not burn. Pour the soup, reheated if it has cooled, into four bowls and then top each with a spoonful of the tadka, which diners should stir into the soup. Serve straight away with slices of naan on the side, if you like.

Cream of chicken soup is probably one of the most popular soups – it is proper hug-in-a-mug stuff and, although you can buy good store-bought versions, it is worth taking the time to make it yourself. You can use leftover cooked chicken in place of the fresh chicken, if you prefer, adding it to the pan with the stock and reducing the cooking time to 15 minutes. You can also replace the chicken thighs with breasts, but thigh meat does give the soup a stronger flavour.

Cream of chicken soup

1 tablespoon olive oil
1 onion, thinly sliced
500 g/1 lb. 2 oz. boneless, skinless chicken thighs
2 garlic cloves, sliced
250 ml/1 cup white wine
1 litre/4 cups chicken or vegetable stock
250 ml/1 cup milk or double/heavy cream
salt and freshly ground black pepper
chopped fresh tarragon, to garnish (optional)

Serves 4–6

In a large saucepan, heat the oil and sauté the onion until soft and translucent.

Cut the chicken thighs in half and add to the saucepan. Sear the chicken thigh pieces so that they are lightly golden brown on all sides. If your saucepan is too small, you can cook the chicken in batches.

Add the garlic to the saucepan and cook for a few minutes more.

Add the wine to the saucepan and simmer for a few minutes to burn off the alcohol, then add the stock, season with salt and pepper, and simmer the soup for 30 minutes. Add the milk or cream to the saucepan and remove from the heat.

Remove half of the chicken from the saucepan using a slotted spoon and cut into small pieces. Set aside.

Blend the remaining soup in a blender or food processor until smooth, or use a stick blender, then return to the pan and add back in the cooked chopped chicken.

Heat the soup and taste for seasoning, adding more salt and pepper if needed. Serve piping hot with a sprinkling of black pepper and some freshly chopped tarragon, if you like.

Who doesn't love a lasagne? It is one of the most popular dishes. This soup takes all of the elements – rich beef Bolognese, creamy white sauce, mozzarella and lasagne pasta sheets – and makes them into a satisfying soup. You can use soup pasta rather than lasagne, if you prefer.

Lasagne soup

1 tablespoon olive oil
400 g/14 oz. minced/ground beef (low fat)
1 tablespoon Worcestershire sauce
15 g/1 tablespoon butter
1 onion, finely chopped
2 garlic cloves, finely chopped
1 large carrot, peeled and grated
400-g/14-oz. can chopped tomatoes
250 ml/1 cup red wine
70 g/5 tablespoons tomato purée/paste
1 litre/4 cups beef stock
4 sheets of lasagne pasta
1 ball of mozzarella (about 150 g/5 oz.), cut into pieces
salt and freshly ground black pepper
fresh basil leaves, to serve
freshly grated Parmesan, to serve

FOR THE CHEESE SAUCE
60 g/4 tablespoons butter
50 g/heaping 1/3 cup plain/all-purpose flour
300 ml/1¼ cups milk
pinch of freshly grated nutmeg
100 g/1 cup plus 2 tablespoons grated Cheddar
50 g/2/3 cup grated Parmesan

Serves 6

Heat the olive oil in a large saucepan over a medium heat, add the beef and fry until browned and cooked through, stirring all the time. Add the Worcestershire sauce and cook for a further minute, then season well with salt and pepper. Remove the beef using a slotted spoon and drain on paper towels to remove as much fat as possible. Set aside.

Melt the butter in a frying pan/skillet and fry the onion over a gentle heat until soft and translucent. Add the garlic and sauté until lightly golden brown. Add the carrot and sauté for a few minutes until it starts to soften, then return the meat to the pan and add the tomatoes, wine, tomato purée and beef stock. Season with salt and pepper and simmer for about 30 minutes until the sauce thickens. It will still be a very liquid soupy consistency, unlike a traditional ragù.

Break the lasagne sheets into pieces and add to the soup, adding more stock or water if the soup is too thick. Simmer for about 10 minutes until the pasta is soft.

Meanwhile, for the cheese sauce, melt the butter in a clean saucepan over a gentle heat and whisk in the flour to form a roux. Cook for a few minutes, then slowly add the milk, whisking constantly, until you have a thick but pourable sauce. Season with a good grate of nutmeg, salt and pepper, then add the Cheddar and Parmesan. Whisk until melted. Remove from the heat and cover the surface with cling film/plastic wrap to prevent a skin from forming. Keep warm.

When you are ready to serve, pour the soup into bowls, and add the mozzarella. Make sure that each bowl has some of the pasta in it. Pour over some of the cheese sauce and top with fresh basil and freshly grated Parmesan to serve.

Molten Comté, with its nutty, earthy taste and creamy texture, is the ideal choice for these oozing toasts that soak up the rich broth of the onion soup to perfection. This is a comfort food classic.

French onion soup with Comté toasts

25 g/2 tablespoons unsalted butter
3 tablespoons olive oil
1 kg/2¼ lb. large onions, very thinly sliced
250 ml/1 cup dry white wine
1 litre/4 cups rich beef stock
pinch of freshly grated nutmeg
a small handful of fresh thyme sprigs
2 fresh bay leaves
75 ml/⅓ cup good-quality Madeira
1 day-old baguette or other crusty bread, cut into slices
1 garlic clove, peeled
150 g/1¼ cups grated Comté
salt and freshly ground black pepper

Serves 4

Melt the butter in a heavy-based pan or flameproof casserole and add the oil. Add the onions and season with salt. Cook over a low heat, stirring occasionally, for at least 45 minutes until they have reduced right down to a golden, sticky mass.

Add the wine and bubble, stirring, for a minute, then add the beef stock, a good grating of nutmeg and the herbs. Simmer for about 20 minutes, then add the Madeira and bubble for 5 minutes more. Check the seasoning and spoon into four small ovenproof bowls or dishes.

Preheat the grill/broiler to high.

Toast the slices of crusty bread and rub one side all over with the peeled garlic clove. Put the toasts on top of the bowls so that they cover the surface of the soup. Sprinkle with lots and lots of cheese and put on a baking sheet under the grill until the soup is bubbling and the cheese toasts are melted and golden. Serve straight away.

This Hungarian dish is always popular in the mountains, where it makes a hearty meal after an energetic day on the slopes and trails. There is a healthy kick of paprika with the added richness of sour cream, which helps to make this such a warming and comforting dish. This is also delicious made with pork instead of beef – use a slow-cook cut such as shoulder/butt and cut it into large chunks.

Goulash soup with sour cream

olive oil, for frying
100 g/3¾ oz. smoked streaky/fatty bacon, finely chopped
1 kg/2¼ lb. braising steak or beef shin, cut into 2.5-cm/1-inch chunks
2 heaped tablespoons plain/all-purpose flour
2 large onions, thinly sliced
2 red (bell) peppers, deseeded and sliced
3 garlic cloves, crushed
5 juniper berries, crushed
2 bay leaves
1 tablespoon sweet smoked paprika
½ tablespoon hot paprika
2 teaspoons caraway seeds
2 tablespoons tomato purée/paste
1 tablespoon red wine vinegar
1.2 litres/5 cups good beef stock
300 g/10½ oz. waxy potatoes, cut into chunks
2 beetroot/beets, cut into chunks
salt and freshly ground black pepper
chopped fresh parsley and sour cream, to serve

Serves 6

Heat a good layer of olive oil in a flameproof casserole or large saucepan and fry the bacon over a medium heat until starting to colour. Remove with a slotted spoon and set aside.

Dust the beef in the flour with plenty of seasoning, then brown in batches over a high heat in the same pan, adding more oil if necessary. Remove and set aside with the bacon.

Add a little more oil to the pan and add the onions and (bell) peppers. Cook for 10 minutes until softened and the onions start to colour. Add the garlic, juniper, bay and spices, and fry for a few minutes before adding the tomato purée, vinegar and stock.

Return the beef and bacon to the pan and season well. Bring to a simmer, then cover and cook for 2–2½ hours until the beef is starting to become really tender.

Add the potatoes and beetroot to the pan and simmer, with the lid off, until the vegetables are tender.

Stir in the parsley and serve in large warmed bowls with generous dollops of sour cream.

French onion soup is normally made using an Alpine white wine, but this version, popular in British pubs, uses ale instead. It is buttery and sweet, but with the bitter balance of a good full-flavoured strong ale.

Ale, caramelized onion & thyme soup

40 g/3 tablespoons butter
3 large onions, thinly sliced
2 large garlic cloves, crushed
20 g/2 tablespoons dark muscovado/dark brown sugar
200 ml/¾ cup ale
800 ml/3⅓ cups beef stock
2 tablespoons Dijon mustard
3 sprigs of fresh thyme
a handful of chopped fresh parsley
salt and freshly ground black pepper

FOR THE ROUX (OPTIONAL)
30 g/2 tablespoons butter
1 tablespoon plain/all-purpose flour

TO SERVE
6 slices of baguette
olive oil, for brushing
grated Gruyère cheese, or other strong hard cheese

Serves 6

Melt the butter in a heavy-based saucepan, add the onions and cook over a gentle heat until very soft and reduced in volume. They need to be silky, and with no resistance at all – this will take 20–25 minutes. Add the garlic and brown sugar and cook for a few more minutes to allow the onions to take on a deep golden colour, but do not let them crisp.

Pour over the ale and stock, then add the mustard and fresh thyme. If your thyme is of the 'stalky' variety, pick off as many of the little leaves as possible, but add the stalks to impart their flavour, and pull them out before you serve. If you are using soft summer thyme, roughly chop and add it all. Simmer for about 10 minutes to allow all the flavours to infuse. By this time, the onions should be as soft as butter and have no resistance to the bite.

To thicken the soup a little, make a roux. Gently melt the butter in a small saucepan, then remove the pan from the heat and stir in the flour. A little at a time, add the roux mixture to the simmering soup, stirring all the time to prevent lumps. This will gradually thicken the soup just enough for it to be slightly syrupy. (It is not a thick soup, but the roux adds texture and makes it slightly more hearty. If you are cooking for someone who doesn't eat wheat, it can be left out altogether.) Season the soup with salt and plenty of freshly ground black pepper, then stir in the chopped parsley.

Preheat the oven to 180°C (350°F) Gas 4. Brush the baguette slices with a little olive oil and bake until golden brown.

Preheat the grill/broiler to high.

Ladle the soup into heatproof bowls, place a slice of the baked bread on top and scatter with a generous amount of Gruyère. Place under the grill to melt the cheese, then serve.

This delicious, creamy soup is wonderfully comforting. If you have any leftover ham hock, tear it into bite-size pieces and add to the soup before seasoning and simmer a little while to infuse the flavours. Alternatively, just scatter some good chopped ham on top as a garnish.

Creamy leek & potato soup with ham hock

50 g/3½ tablespoons butter
4 leeks, whites only, sliced
4 potatoes, peeled and diced
800 ml/3⅓ cups chicken or vegetable stock
400 ml/1⅔ cups whole milk
a good slug of double/heavy cream
cooked ham, shredded (optional)
salt and freshly ground black pepper

TO GARNISH
a small handful of chopped fresh parsley
a small handful of snipped fresh chives

Serves 6–8

Melt the butter in a large saucepan and add the leeks and potatoes. Cook for a few minutes, until the butter has been absorbed and the vegetables have softened. Pour in the stock and milk and simmer for 15–20 minutes, until the potatoes and leeks are tender.

Draw the pan off the heat and use a stick blender to blend the soup until it is silky smooth. Stir in the cream and add the ham. Season well with salt and pepper.

To serve, ladle the soup into chunky bowls and garnish with a sprinkling of fresh herbs.

A particularly beautiful savoy cabbage was the inspiration for this soup, but you can make it your own with your favourite green leafy vegetables when they are in season – try sweetheart cabbage and spring greens when available. Use a nice big heavy-based pan to slowly cook and hold the heat evenly through the soup, and cut all your vegetables to about the same size so they cook evenly.

Puy lentil & bacon soup with seasonal greens

2–3 tablespoons olive oil
150 g/5 oz. bacon lardons or thick-cut dry cured bacon cut into matchsticks
1 small onion, chopped
4 garlic cloves, crushed
1 leek, sliced
1 celery stick, sliced
2 carrots, peeled and sliced
¼ celeriac/celery root, peeled and diced
¼ swede/rutabaga, peeled and diced
125 g/⅔ cup Puy lentils, rinsed and drained
1.3 litres/5½ cups vegetable stock
400-g/14-oz. can chopped tomatoes
11½ tablespoons tomato purée/paste
¼ small savoy cabbage or other greens (cut as a chiffonade, long and very fine)
a small handful of chopped fresh parsley
a small handful of chopped fresh thyme
salt and freshly ground black pepper

Serves 6–8

Put the olive oil in a large heavy-based saucepan, add the bacon, onion and garlic and cook until the onion is softened and the bacon is just cooked.

Add the leek, celery, carrots, celeriac and swede to the pan, along with the Puy lentils. Stir to coat all the vegetables with the oil so that they absorb a little and glisten slightly, then pour over the stock and chopped tomatoes and season with salt and pepper. Put the lid on the pan and simmer very gently for about 15 minutes – you do not to have each element of this soup holding its own.

Draw the pan off the heat and stir in the tomato purée, greens and chopped fresh herbs. Return to the heat and simmer until the greens are just tender but still retain a little crunch.

Ladle the soup into rustic bowls, to serve.

Jerk paste has the most amazing fiery flavour and immediately transports us to Caribbean holidays, so it's an ideal ingredient to bring a bit of heat to our winter meals. It can be very fiery, so take care not to add too much, otherwise the soup can be overpoweringly hot.

Caribbean sweet potato & coconut soup

2 tablespoons olive oil
1 onion, finely chopped
2 garlic cloves, finely chopped
1 teaspoon jerk paste
1 tablespoon tomato purée/paste
600–700 g/1 lb. 5 oz.–1 lb. 9 oz. sweet potato, peeled and cut into chunks
700 ml/scant 3 cups chicken or vegetable stock
400-ml/14-oz. can coconut milk
salt and freshly ground black pepper
toasted strips of coconut, to serve

Serves 4–6

In a large saucepan, heat the oil over a gentle heat and add the onion. Fry until soft and translucent. Add the garlic and cook for a few minutes until it is lightly golden brown. Add the jerk paste and fry to infuse the flavours. How much depends on how hot you like your food. Jerk paste is generally very fiery so take care not to add too much unless you like very hot spices.

Add the tomato purée and the sweet potatoes and cook for a few minutes more, then add the stock and the coconut milk. Simmer until the potatoes are soft; 20–30 minutes.

Place the soup in a blender or food processor and blend until smooth, or use a stick blender. Season with salt and pepper to taste.

Serve hot with toasted coconut and some extra black pepper on top.

HEARTY SOUPS

Vietnamese cooking is fresh and fragrant with the perfect combination of sweet, salty and savoury. Pho is a simple yet warming broth in which you poach vegetables, adding seasonings of your choosing. If you can find Thai basil, use it for an authentic taste. Omit the fish sauce for veggies.

Vietnamese vegetable pho

1 tablespoon olive oil
1 onion, thinly sliced
1 garlic clove, thinly sliced
2.5-cm/1-inch piece of ginger, peeled and thinly sliced
2 star anise
1 teaspoon ground cinnamon
½ teaspoon dried chilli flakes/hot red pepper flakes
1 tablespoon chopped fresh coriander/cilantro
1 tablespoon chopped fresh basil (Thai basil if available)
1 tablespoon soy sauce
1 tablespoon fish sauce
1 litre/4 cups vegetable stock
1 carrot, peeled
1 pak choi/bok choy
2 spring onions/scallions, thinly sliced
150 g/5 oz. mushrooms, sliced
freshly squeezed juice of 2 limes
2 teaspoons white sugar
80 g/3 oz. ramen noodles
bahn mi, to serve (optional)

Serves 4

In a large saucepan, heat the oil and fry the onion, garlic and ginger slices until the onion is soft. Add the star anise, cinnamon and dried chilli flakes to the saucepan and fry for a further minute. Add the coriander, basil, soy sauce, fish sauce and stock and simmer for about 10 minutes.

Thinly slice the carrot into ribbons using a swivel peeler and add to the saucepan. Trim the pak choi and slice lengthways. Add the carrot, pak choi, spring onions and mushrooms to the saucepan. Pour in the lime juice, add the sugar and simmer for 5 minutes.

Add the noodles and cook for a further 5 minutes.

Remove the star anise and then pour the soup into four bowls to serve.

Serve with Vietnamese-style bahn mi for a heartier meal, if you like.

Fondues & Melted Cheese

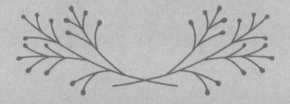

Food trends come and go and cider has for the last few years enjoyed something of a renaissance. You can now find a whole range of flavoured ciders in your local supermarket. A good brut cider works well here, You can, of course, serve any bread, but making pretzels is such fun – give it a try.

Cider fondue with pretzels

1 garlic clove, peeled
180 ml/¾ cup (hard) cider, ideally dry/brut
1 tablespoon cider vinegar
200 g/1¾ cups grated Gruyère
200 g/generous 2 cups grated Cheddar
200 g/1¾ cups grated Monterey Jack or Gouda
1 tablespoon plain/all-purpose flour
2 teaspoons mustard powder
2 tablespoons apple liqueur, such as Calvados (optional)
a selection of deli-style dippers, such as dill pickles, salami or pastrami slices, to serve

FOR THE PRETZELS
300 ml/1¼ cups warm water
1½ teaspoons dried active yeast
1 teaspoon salt
1 tablespoon caster/granulated sugar
1 tablespoon olive oil, plus extra for oiling the bowl
500 g/3½ cups bread flour, plus extra for dusting
125 g/½ cup bicarbonate of soda/baking soda
a handful of coarse sea salt

Serves 6

For the pretzels, combine half the water with the yeast, salt, sugar and oil, and stir to dissolve the yeast. Gradually work in the flour and enough of the remaining water to form a soft dough. Knead on a lightly floured surface for 5–10 minutes until smooth. Place in a lightly oiled bowl, cover with cling film/plastic wrap and rest for 30 minutes.

Cut the dough into 12 equal pieces. Roll each one to a thin sausage 40–50 cm/16–20 inches in length. Bring the ends together to form a circle overlapping at the top, then twist around each other once, bringing the ends back towards you. Press the ends firmly onto the bottom of the circle, a little apart from each other to form a classic pretzel shape. Cover with a clean kitchen towel and allow to rest for 15 minutes.

Preheat the oven to 200°C (400°F) Gas 6 and line 2 baking sheets with baking paper.

Put the bicarbonate of soda in a large pan with 2 litres/8 cups cold water. Bring slowly to the boil. Carefully immerse 2–3 pretzels at a time into the water and cook for 30 seconds. Remove with a slotted spoon, shake off as much water as you can, place on the prepared baking sheets and scatter with salt. Repeat with the remaining pretzels. Bake in the preheated oven for 15 minutes until golden. Cool on a wire rack.

For the fondue, rub the peeled garlic around the inside of your fondue pot and place on a medium heat on the stovetop. Pour in the cider and bring to the boil. Combine the cheeses in a bowl with the flour and mustard powder, and gradually stir into the cider. Continue stirring until the cheese is melted. Season to taste and stir in the liqueur if using. Place the pot on the tabletop burner and serve with dippers and the pretzels.

The Italian version of fondue is a speciality of the Valle d'Aosta in the northwest of the country, where cold winters are common. It is made with Fontina cheese, enriched with egg yolks, then scattered decadently with shavings of white truffle from neighbouring Piedmont. If you don't have a truffle to hand, a sprinkling of truffle oil will give a hint of the prized fragrance.

Fonduta

½ teaspoon cornflour/cornstarch
250 ml/1 cup milk
400 g/14 oz. Fontina, chopped
35 g/2¼ tablespoons unsalted butter, melted
4 egg yolks
freshly ground white pepper
1 white truffle (optional) or truffle oil

TO SERVE
steamed spring vegetables such as baby carrots, baby leeks, baby turnips, asparagus, fennel and mangetout, cut into bite-sized pieces if necessary
cubes of fresh bread

Serves 6

Put the cornflour into a small bowl, add 1 tablespoon of the milk and stir until dissolved – this is called 'slaking'. Put the remaining milk into the top section of a double boiler, then add the cheese and slaked cornflour.

Set over a saucepan of simmering water and heat, stirring constantly, until the cheese has melted. Stir in the butter and remove from the heat.

Put the egg yolks into a bowl and whisk lightly. Whisk in a few tablespoons of the hot cheese mixture to warm the yolks. Pour this mixture back into the double boiler, stirring vigorously. Return the saucepan to the heat and continue stirring until the mixture thickens.

To serve, ladle the cheese mixture into warmed bowls and sprinkle with freshly ground white pepper and shavings of truffle, if using. Alternatively, sprinkle with a few drops of truffle oil. Serve the bowls surrounded by the prepared vegetables and cubes of fresh bread for dipping.

Manchego is a hard sheep's milk cheese with a unique flavour – zesty, nutty and fruity all at once with a slightly crumbly texture. It melts well, but is even better when blended with a semi-soft cheese. Stir a little romesco sauce into the pot to serve and enjoy with a selection of tapas – charcuterie, Spanish tortilla and crusty bread – to bring a bit of Spanish warmth to your winter.

Spanish cheese fondue with romesco

250 g/3 cups grated Manchego
250 g/generous 2 cups grated Mahon, Taleggio or Provolone
2 teaspoons cornflour/cornstarch
175 ml/¾ cup Spanish white wine, such as Albariño
1 tablespoon sherry vinegar
a mixed platter of Spanish charcuterie, tortilla cubes, bread and a tomato salad, to serve

FOR THE ROMESCO SAUCE
75 g/⅔ cup roasted salted almonds, roughly chopped
1 large garlic clove, chopped
75 g/2½ oz. roasted red (bell) pepper, drained and chopped
2 tablespoons sun-dried/sun-blushed tomatoes, drained
4 tablespoons extra virgin olive oil
1 tablespoon red wine vinegar
½ teaspoon caster/granulated sugar
½ teaspoon smoked paprika
¼ teaspoon Espelette or cayenne pepper
salt and freshly ground black pepper

Serves 4

First make the romesco sauce. Place all the ingredients into a small food processor and blend together until really smooth. Adjust seasonings and store in a screw-top jar until required.

To prepare the fondue, combine the cheeses in a bowl and add a little pepper, stir well. Blend the cornflour with 1 tablespoon of the wine and set aside.

Heat the remaining wine in your fondue pot on the stovetop until boiling. Gradually add the cheeses, stirring constantly until smooth and bubbling. Stir in the cornflour and sherry vinegar and cook for 2 minutes until thickened.

If you like, stir a couple of tablespoons of the romesco into the fondue now. Alternatively transfer the pot to your tabletop burner and arrange the charcuterie, bread, tortilla cubes and tomato salad on platters and serve with small bowls of romesco sauce.

Use a mild blue cheese such as the blended cheese Cambozola, a Danish blue or Gorgonzola for this dish. If you prefer to serve this as a more traditional fondue then go for it, but it does work well on fries. It is also good with ripe pears and wedges of crisp Little Gem/Boston lettuce.

Blue cheese fondue with potato fries

1 kg/2¼ lb. Maris Piper, Yukon Gold or King Edward potatoes
2 tablespoons olive oil
250 g/9 oz. Cambozola, diced
200 g/7 oz. Gruyère, grated
1 tablespoon white vinegar
1 tablespoon cornflour/cornstarch
1 garlic clove, crushed
1 teaspoon freshly chopped thyme
150 ml/⅔ cup light blonde beer
3 tablespoons single/light cream
salt and freshly ground black pepper
chargrilled bread or Little Gem/Boston lettuce quarters, ripe pear wedges, to serve (optional)

FOR THE PICKLED RED ONION RINGS
125 ml/½ cup cider vinegar
30 g/2½ tablespoons granulated sugar
1 teaspoon salt
1 red onion, thinly sliced
1 garlic clove, thinly sliced
a pinch of black or pink peppercorns

Serves 6

First make the pickled onion rings. Place the vinegar, 125 ml/½ cup water, the sugar and salt in a small saucepan and bring to the boil over a low heat. Let it boil for 1 minute, then remove from the heat. Meanwhile, place the onion, garlic and peppercorns into a sterilized 350-ml/12-oz. jar. Pour the hot pickling mixture directly over the onion and seal the jar with a vinegar-safe lid. Cool and set aside until required.

Preheat the oven to 200°C (400°F) Gas 6 and line a large baking sheet with baking paper.

Cut the potatoes into thin fries no more than 5 mm/¼ inch thick and place on the prepared baking sheet. Add half the oil, salt and pepper and stir well. Bake in the preheated oven for 45–50 minutes, stirring from time to time, until crisp and golden.

Meanwhile, combine the cheeses with a little pepper. Stir the vinegar and cornflour together until smooth.

About 10 minutes before the potatoes are cooked, heat the remaining oil in a fondue pot on the stovetop and gently fry the garlic and thyme over a low heat for 3 minutes until softened. Add the beer and cream and bring to the boil, then stir in the cheese until melted. Stir in the cornflour and vinegar mixture and simmer for 1–2 minutes until thickened.

Arrange the potato fries on plates or in bowls and spoon over the sauce. Serve with the pickled onion rings and some chargrilled bread. Or alternatively, serve as a fondue with the fries, pickles, lettuce and pears.

Directly translated, croûte au fromage nature *means simply 'plain cheese on toast'. Definitely sounds more appetizing in French, and it is more interesting than the name suggests. It was, no doubt, introduced as a way to use leftovers from a fondue or just stale bread and cheese, but here the bread is soaked in wine to soften it and help the cheese, which is grated on and around the bread, to melt more easily. Hugely popular in the mountain regions of France.*

Croûte au fromage nature

butter, for greasing
2 large slices of sourdough bread
1 garlic clove, peeled
75 ml/⅓ cup dry white wine
4 slices of pastrami or ham, about 100 g/3½ oz.
300 g/2½ cups grated Gruyère or Emmental
freshly grated nutmeg
2 tablespoons grated Parmesan
salt and freshly ground black pepper

Serves 2–4

Preheat the oven to 220°C (425°F) Gas 7 and butter the inside of a 1.5-litre/1½-quart baking dish.

Griddle the bread slices until charred on both sides, then rub all over with the garlic and place in the prepared dish. Season the bread with a little salt and pepper. Pour the wine into the dish and top the bread with the pastrami or ham. Scatter over the Gruyère or Emmental, some grated nutmeg and the Parmesan. Transfer to the preheated oven and bake for 20 minutes until bubbling and golden.

Variation *If you like, serve the dish topped with a couple of fried eggs, or for those who do not eat meat you can replace it with some sautéed and seasoned spinach.*

This classic raclette dish is traditionally served with boiled new potatoes, cornichons and pickled onions. Here the potatoes are roasted alongside shallots and garlic flavoured with rosemary and bay leaves. Once the vegetables are al dente they are 'smashed', drizzled with more olive oil and roasted again until they have a crispy, golden crust. At this stage they can now be transferred to the table for diners to help themselves and then the melted Raclette is spooned over.

Raclette over roasted potatoes
with garlic, shallots and rosemary

8 garlic cloves, unpeeled
8 small shallots, unpeeled
4 bay leaves, lightly bashed
2 sprigs of fresh rosemary,
   lightly bashed
1 kg/2¼ lb. unpeeled chat potatoes
   or similar floury baby potatoes
4 tablespoons olive oil
200 g/7 oz. Raclette, cut into slices
salt and freshly ground black pepper
caperberries, silverskin/cocktail onions
   and a green salad, to serve

Serves 6

Preheat the oven to 200°C (400°F) Gas 6 and line a roasting pan with baking paper.

Put the garlic cloves, shallots and herbs into a saucepan and cover with cold water. Bring to the boil and simmer for 1 minute. Immediately drain and refresh the vegetables under cold running water. Pat dry and then peel the garlic and shallots, leaving them whole.

Place the potatoes, garlic, shallots, herbs, half the oil and some salt and pepper in the prepared roasting pan and stir so that everything is evenly coated in oil. Cover with foil and cook in the preheated oven for 30 minutes, checking they are al dente. Remove the pan from the oven, discarding the foil and herbs. Using a potato masher, 'smash' the potato mixture so it is roughly mashed. Drizzle over the remaining oil and return to the oven. Roast uncovered for a further 10–15 minutes until crisp and golden.

About 5 minutes before the potatoes are ready, heat the raclette machine or conventional grill/broiler to the highest setting. Place the tray of potatoes on the table for everyone to help themselves. Grill/broil the cheese slices either for 2 minutes or until bubbling and completely melted. Using a wooden spatula, scrape the cheese onto your plate of roasted potatoes and serve with caperberries, silverskin onions and a green salad.

Cosy jumpers, roaring fire, enough melted cheese and wine to sink a battleship – what could be better! This classic fondue uses Swiss Emmental and Gruyère, but you can use Gouda and Comté, if preferred. If you don't have a fondue set, a good cast-iron or copper pot warmed through will keep the fondue warm.

Classic fondue

500 g/1 lb. 2 oz. baby new potatoes
12 asparagus spears
30 g/2 tablespoons butter
2 pears
1 sourdough loaf, cut into 4-cm/1½-inch cubes
285-g/10-oz. jar cornichons and baby pickled onions, drained
2 figs, halved
1 celery stick, cut into 4-cm/1½-inch pieces
salt

FOR THE FONDUE
1 small garlic clove, crushed
freshly grated nutmeg
400 ml/1¾ cups white wine
300 g/2½ cups grated Emmental
300 g/2½ cups grated Gruyère
100 g/generous ¾ cup Cambozola, Taleggio or Dolcelatte, cut into chunks
2 tablespoons brandy
1 tablespoon cornflour/cornstarch, plus extra if needed

Serves 6–8

Boil the potatoes for 12 minutes, or until they are fork tender but not mushy. Drain, season with salt and leave to steam dry.

Fry the asparagus spears in the butter for a few minutes, then let cool.

Quarter the pears, leaving the skin on. Cover with a damp tea/dish towel.

Leave the cubed sourdough open to the air to help it dry out a little.

Pour all the fondue ingredients – except the brandy and cornflour into a large saucepan and gently bring to a simmer, stirring all the time. Season with salt and pepper.

Once the cheese has melted and the wine has started bubbling, turn the heat down.

Make a slurry with the brandy and cornflour and stir into the fondue. Keep it on the heat until the mixture thickens and becomes smooth, then remove from the heat. (If it splits or looks grainy, add another tablespoon cornflour with a little water and stir continuously over the heat to bring it back together.)

Pour the mixture into a fondue pot and place in the middle of the serving board. Add a little freshly grated nutmeg to the top of the fondue for a nice touch.

Add the cornichons and onions to the board in little ramekins, then fill the board with clusters of potatoes, asparagus, pear slices, sourdough cubes, figs and celery. Serve immediately!

Cauliflower cheese has got to be one of the most comforting side dishes ever. This is a fairly traditional version, but the veg has been pre-roasted to give it more depth of flavour and it boasts a herby, garlicky, crunchy topping.

Cauliflower & leek gratin

1 cauliflower head, cut into florets, stalk cut into chunks, leaves reserved

3 leeks, cut into 6-cm/2½-inch chunks

olive oil, for roasting

50 g/3½ tablespoons salted butter

50 g/heaped ⅓ cup plain/all-purpose flour

700 ml/3 cups whole milk

200 g/generous 2 cups grated Cheddar

5 g/¼ oz. each fresh oregano and sage, leaves only

40 g/¾ cup breadcrumbs

10 cloves Confit Garlic (see below)

salt and freshly ground black pepper

Serves 4–6

Preheat the oven to 220°C (425°F) Gas 7.

Add the cauliflower (including the leaves and stalk) and leeks to your largest baking sheet and drizzle with a glug of olive oil and a good pinch of seasoning. Toss to coat, then place on the top shelf of the preheated oven to roast for 30 minutes.

Meanwhile, melt the butter in a medium saucepan set over a medium heat, then add the flour and mix vigorously to combine. Cook for 3–4 minutes until it becomes a 'brown roux' (you want it a nice shade of butterscotch), then add a first splash of the milk and whisk. This will cause it to thicken.

Once that milk has all been absorbed and become stiff, add another glug of milk, and continue to do so, gradually, whisking continuously. Once all the milk is in the pan, gently stir until the sauce thickens; 5 minutes or so. When your sauce has a lovely, custard-like thickness, remove from the heat and fold through three-quarters of the grated cheese. Taste to check for seasoning, you'll probably need to add more salt and pepper. Set aside until the veg is roasted and out of the oven.

Mix the remaining grated cheese with the herbs, breadcrumbs and a pinch more seasoning. This is your topping. Transfer the roasted veg to a baking dish and then pour the cheese sauce on top. Sprinkle over the topping, then add the confit garlic cloves. Bake on the top shelf of the preheated oven for 25 minutes until golden brown, bubbling and crisp.

CONFIT GARLIC

Peel the cloves from 3 bulbs of garlic, and place in a pan with 200ml/scant 1 cup olive oil, a sprig of rosemary and a bay leaf. Place over the lowest possible heat (it should be barely a simmer) for 40 minutes until the cloves are tender but remain uncoloured. Transfer to a sterilized jar and store in the fridge.

Welsh rarebit is so simple to prepare and makes a lovely supper, whether topping toast, a crumpet or, as in this recipe, a savoury waffle. Melted cheese with mustard and tangy Worcestershire sauce served with roasted vine tomatoes and a crisp green salad – what could be better?

Welsh rarebit waffles

200 g/1⅔ cups self-raising/self-rising flour, sifted
3 eggs, separated
250 ml/1 cup milk
70 g/5 tablespoons butter, melted, plus extra for greasing
salt and freshly ground black pepper

FOR THE ROASTED TOMATOES

300 g/1⅔ cups vine cherry tomatoes
1–2 tablespoons olive oil
1 tablespoon balsamic glaze
1 tablespoon caster/granulated sugar

FOR THE TOPPING

300 g/3½ cups grated Cheddar
1 egg
2 teaspoons wholegrain mustard
1 tablespoon Worcestershire sauce, plus extra to serve

an electric or stove-top waffle iron

Serves 6

Preheat the oven to 180°C (350°F) Gas 4.

Begin with the roasted tomatoes. Put the tomatoes in the roasting pan and drizzle with the olive oil, balsamic glaze and caster sugar. Season with salt and pepper and roast in the preheated oven for 20–30 minutes until the tomatoes are soft and their juices start to run. Keep warm until you are ready to serve.

To make the waffle batter, put the flour, egg yolks, milk and melted butter into a large mixing bowl. Whisk until you have a smooth batter. Season with salt and pepper. In a separate mixing bowl, whisk the egg whites to stiff peaks and then gently fold into the batter a third at a time.

Preheat the waffle iron and grease with a little butter.

Ladle some of the batter into the preheated waffle iron and cook for 2–3 minutes until golden brown. Keep warm while you cook the remaining batter and are ready to serve.

Preheat the grill/broiler to high.

Put all the topping ingredients into a bowl and mix. Spread a large spoonful of the topping mixture over each waffle and place under the hot grill for a few minutes until the cheese melts and starts to turn golden brown. Watch carefully to make sure that the rarebit topping and waffle do not burn, turning the grill heat down if required.

Splash the tops of the waffles with a few drops of Worcestershire sauce and serve immediately with the roasted tomatoes on top.

FONDUES & MELTED CHEESE

TOASTIES & JACKETS

Melted cheese is complemented by sour or tangy ingredients that cut through the richness. Here, kimchi, a spiced Korean condiment of fermented pickled cabbage, does just that to perfection. The combination may sound strange at first, but it's fantastic. There's a good reason why kimchi is taking off around the world!

Kimchi & Monterey Jack toastie

4 slices of white bread, crusts removed
unsalted butter, softened
60 g/½ cup kimchi
150 g/1¾ cups grated mild cheese, such as Monterey Jack or mild Cheddar

Serves 2

Butter each of the bread slices on one side and set aside. Pat the kimchi dry with paper towels to remove excess moisture and chop.

Without turning the heat on, put two slices of the bread in a large, heavy-based non-stick frying pan/skillet, butter-side down. If you can only fit one slice in your pan, you'll need to cook one sandwich at a time. Top with half the kimchi and sprinkle over half the grated cheese in an even layer. Cover each with another bread slice, butter-side up.

Turn the heat to medium and cook the first side for 3–5 minutes until it turns a deep golden colour, pressing gently with a spatula. Carefully turn with the spatula and cook on the second side for 2–3 minutes, or until deep golden brown all over.

Remove from the frying pan, transfer to a plate and cut in half. Let cool for a few minutes before serving.

Note *Vegetarians should note that kimchi often contains fish as part of the seasoning.*

Thin slices of Brie melt more successfully than thick ones, so a good tip with this recipe is to slice the cheese when it is chilled (which is easier), then bring the slices to room temperature before using in the sandwich. Also, remove the rind because it does not melt well. Feel free to substitute whole-wheat bread if walnut bread is not available.

Brie & apple-cranberry toastie

4–8 slices of walnut bread, depending on size of loaf
unsalted butter, softened
about 180g/6 oz. ripe chilled Brie, rind removed, thinly sliced or finely diced

FOR THE APPLE-CRANBERRY SAUCE
300 g/3 cups cranberries, fresh or frozen
juice of 1 orange
1 small tart cooking apple, such as Cox, peeled and diced
about 3 tablespoons caster/granulated sugar or more to taste

Serves 2

For the apple-cranberry sauce, combine all the ingredients in a saucepan over a low heat. Stir the mixture often, until the sugar dissolves and the cranberries begin to pop and disintegrate. If the mixture is too dry, add a small amount of water. Cover and simmer gently until the cranberries are tender and the mixture has a jam-like consistency; keep checking to see if the mixture is too dry – if it is, add water bit-by-bit to prevent the mixture from thickening and burning. Taste and adjust the sweetness to your liking. Set aside until needed.

Butter the bread slices on one side.

Without turning the heat on, place two slices of the bread in a large, heavy-based, non-stick frying pan/skillet, butter-side down. If you can't fit two slices side-by-side in the pan, you'll need to cook them in two batches. Spread the slices generously with some of the apple-cranberry sauce, then top with Brie slices. Cover with the remaining bread slices, butter-side up.

Turn the heat to medium and cook the first side for 3–5 minutes until it turns a deep golden colour, pressing gently with a spatula. Carefully turn with the spatula and cook on the second side for 2–3 minutes, or until deep golden brown all over.

Remove from the frying pan, transfer to a plate and cut in half. Let cool for a few minutes before serving along with extra apple-cranberry sauce.

Note *Leftover apple-cranberry sauce can be kept in the refrigerator in a sealed container.*

The authentic version of this sandwich calls for melted cheese to top the meat and onions, so grilling it is a departure from tradition. The cheese can either be Swiss cheese or processed cheese, but this recipe uses both. The dill pickle is not part of the real thing, but it adds a welcome tang and crunch to this substantial classic.

Philly cheesesteak sandwich

1 ciabatta or 2 long white rolls
3 tablespoons spreadable processed cheese, such as Dairylea or Kraft
vegetable oil, for brushing
6–8 slices of Emmental or Swiss cheese
2 large gherkins/pickles, thinly sliced lengthwise, plus extra to serve

FOR THE ONIONS
2 large onions, thinly sliced
15 g/1 tablespoon unsalted butter
2 tablespoons vegetable oil
salt and freshly ground black pepper

FOR THE BEEF
1 tablespoon vegetable oil
350 g/12½ oz. minute/cube steak, thinly sliced
salt and freshly ground black pepper

Serves 2

For the onions, in a frying pan/skillet, combine the onions with the butter and vegetable oil. Cook over a medium heat, stirring occasionally, until deep golden brown, about 10 minutes. Season lightly and transfer to a small bowl.

For the beef, in the same pan, add the oil and heat. When hot but not smoking, add the beef and cook for 2–3 minutes, stirring often, until cooked through. Season and set aside.

Cut the ciabatta in half at the middle to obtain two even pieces, and slice these in half widthways. Take the bottom halves and spread the insides with processed cheese. With a small brush, coat the outsides of the bread, tops and bottoms, lightly with oil.

Put the top (plain) halves of bread, oil-side down, in a large, heavy-based, non-stick frying pan. Depending on the size of your pan, you may need to cook one sandwich at a time. Arrange half the Emmental slices on top of these bread slices, then top each with half the beef and half the onions. Cover with the processed cheese-coated bottom halves, oil-side up, to enclose the sandwich.

Turn the heat to medium and cook for 3–5 minutes until deep golden, pressing gently with a large spatula. Carefully turn with the spatula and cook on the other side for 2–3 minutes more, or until deep golden brown all over.

Remove from the pan and cut in half. Let cool for a few minutes before serving with gherkins.

This recipe is basically loaded scrambled eggs sandwiched between two crispy wraps, what's not to like about that? It uses only one pan, and it's a great dish for the whole family, because it's an eat-with-your-hands meal that you can enjoy while lounging in the kitchen on a chilly Saturday morning, or make it for lunch when you want something warming and satisfying.

Weekend quesadillas

olive oil, for frying
100 g/3½ oz. mushrooms, thinly sliced
100 g/3½ oz. bacon lardons
50 g/2 oz. spinach
4 eggs
40 g/scant ½ cup grated cheese
4 tortilla wraps, 20-cm/8-inch diameter
salt and freshly ground black pepper

Serves 4

Add a drizzle of oil to a medium or large, non-stick frying pan/skillet and set over a high heat. Once hot, add the mushrooms and fry for 3 minutes until softening and starting to colour slightly. Add the lardons to the pan and continue to fry for 3–5 minutes until the bacon is golden and the mushrooms are well browned.

Next, add the spinach and stir it through the mushroom mixture until it wilts – this should only take a minute. Scoop all of the cooked items out of the pan and on to a plate, then wipe the pan clean with some paper towels (don't wash it as you're about to use it again).

Next, whisk the eggs in a bowl, season well, then add the mushroom mixture and briefly mix. The residual heat might start to cook the eggs slightly, but that's fine.

The grated cheese is used to create a barrier for the egg mix, so sprinkle the cheese in a 2.5-cm/1-inch thick ring around the edge of two of the tortillas. Place one of these tortillas in the frying pan, spoon half the egg mixture into the centre and spread it up to the ring of cheese. Gently place a plain tortilla on top and fry for 2–3 minutes, until the egg is starting to set and the base tortilla is crispy. Using a spatula and some confidence, flip the quesadilla over and fry on the other side for 2–3 minutes.

Transfer to a board and repeat with the remaining ingredients to make the second quesadilla.

To serve, slice up the quesadillas like a pizza and enjoy.

Lasagne is a great prepare-ahead dish. This version replaces the pasta with layers of fluffy jacket potato, making it a hybrid of lasagne and moussaka.

Lasagne layered baked potato

4 large baking potatoes
salt

FOR THE MEAT FILLING

1 onion, finely chopped
2 garlic cloves, crushed
1–2 tablespoons olive oil
400 g/14 oz. lean minced/ground beef
1 carrot, peeled and coarsely grated
400-g/14-oz. can chopped tomatoes
70 g/2½ oz. tomato purée/paste
250 ml/1 cup red wine
500 ml/2 cups beef stock

FOR THE CHEESE SAUCE

30 g/2 tablespoons butter
2 tablespoons plain/all-purpose flour
200 ml/scant 1 cup milk
120 g/1⅓ cups grated Cheddar, plus extra for sprinkling
freshly grated nutmeg
salt and freshly ground black pepper

6 chef's rings that are about the diameter of your potatoes

6 pieces of foil, larger than the chef's rings

Serves 6

Prepare the meat filling the day before you want to serve. In a large pan, fry the onion and garlic in the olive oil until the onion has softened and started to turn light golden brown. Add the beef to the pan and fry until the meat has browned. Add all the remaining ingredients and simmer for 1 hour until the sauce has thickened and most of the liquid has evaporated. Leave to cool, then store in the refrigerator overnight.

Preheat the oven to 200°C (400°F) Gas 6.

Prick the skin of the potatoes and rub with salt. Bake in the preheated oven for 1 hour, or until tender. Leave the oven on. Alternatively, cook in the microwave for about 8 minutes.

Meanwhile, prepare the cheese sauce. Heat the butter in a pan over a gentle heat until melted, then add the flour and whisk to incorporate into the butter. Cook for a few minutes, taking care that the mixture does not burn. Whisk in the milk, a little at a time. Add the cheese to the sauce and whisk over a gentle heat until the cheese has melted and the sauce has thickened. Season with salt, pepper and a little nutmeg. Cool.

Reduce the oven to 180°C (350°F) Gas 4. Cut the cooked potatoes into round discs. Grease the chef's rings and a baking sheet with a little butter. Fold one piece of foil up around the edges of each chef's ring. Place on a baking sheet. Carefully place a large disc of potato in the bottom of each ring. The potato should fill the ring. Place a spoonful of the meat on top of the potato and cover with a spoonful of cheese sauce. Place another layer of potato on top and repeat with the meat and cheese layers. Sprinkle over a little extra grated cheese.

Bake in the oven for 15–20 minutes until the top is golden. Remove from the oven and leave to cool for a few minutes. Remove the foil, place each ring on a serving plate then lift up the ring. Serve with salad.

Aubergine/eggplant roasted with olive oil until crisp makes a fantastic potato topping. In this recipe, it's roasted with tomatoes, garlic and onion, providing a boost of warmth from sunny Mediterranean flavours. Topped with crème fraîche, pine nuts and a drizzle of harissa, this makes a perfect lunch dish. It is important to use a harissa that is oily so that it is easy to spoon over.

Jacket stuffed with aubergine,
harissa, crème fraîche & toasted pine nuts

2 large baking potatoes
½ small onion, thinly sliced
1 garlic clove, thinly sliced
½ large red chilli/chile, deseeded and finely chopped
1 aubergine/eggplant, cut into 3-cm/1¼-inch cubes
10 cherry tomatoes, halved
olive oil, for roasting
2–3 tablespoons olive oil
2 tablespoons pine nuts
2 tablespoons crème fraîche
1 tablespoon harissa paste
salt

Serves 2

Preheat the oven to 200°C (400°F) Gas 6.

Prick the skin of the potatoes and rub with salt. Bake in the preheated oven for 1 hour, or until tender. Alternatively, cook in the microwave for about 8 minutes, or until tender.

Meanwhile, place the onion, garlic and chilli in the bottom of a roasting pan, spreading out evenly, and cover with the aubergine and tomatoes Drizzle with the olive oil so that all the aubergine is coated in oil. Bake for 30–40 minutes until the aubergine has started to crisp and the rest of the vegetables are soft. Check halfway through cooking and drizzle over a little more olive oil if needed.

Meanwhile, place the pine nuts in a dry frying pan/skillet and toast over a gentle heat until they start to turn golden brown. Stir all the time as they can burn easily.

When you are ready to serve, cut the potatoes open and place on serving plates. Stir the aubergine mixture and divide between the potatoes. Top each with a large spoonful of crème fraîche and sprinkle over the toasted pine nuts. Drizzle with a little harissa for a spicy kick and serve straight away.

Bacon, Brie and cranberry is a popular sandwich filling, so why not serve it on top of a potato? This one is very quick and easy to make and needs minimum preparation so is a great supper to rustle up after work when you're in need of comfort food. You can use back bacon in place of streaky bacon, if you prefer.

Bacon, Brie & cranberry jackets

1 large baking potato
4 rashers/slices smoked streaky/fatty bacon
15 g/1 tablespoon butter
2 tablespoons cranberry sauce
75 g/2½ oz. ripe Brie
salt and freshly ground black pepper

Serves 1

Preheat the oven to 200°C (400°F) Gas 6.

Prick the skin of the potatoes and rub with salt. Bake in the preheated oven for 1 hour, or until tender. Alternatively, cook in the microwave for about 8 minutes, or until tender.

In a frying/skillet or griddle pan, cook the bacon for about 5 minutes until crisp and golden brown.

Cut the potato in half and scoop out the soft potato middle. Reserve the skins. Place the potato in a bowl and mash with the butter until soft, then season well with salt and pepper. Scoop the potato back into the skins and place in an ovenproof dish or on a baking sheet.

Preheat the grill/broiler to high.

Place two rashers of bacon on each potato half and top with a spoonful of cranberry sauce. Cut the Brie into slices and place on top of each potato half.

Place the potato halves under the grill for 5 minutes until the bacon is cooked and the Brie has melted and is gooey. Serve straight away.

Topped with crisp puff pastry these little pies are a meal in themselves.

Chicken & leek pot pie jackets

4 large baking potatoes
300 g/10½ oz. ready-made puff pastry
1 egg, beaten
flour, for dusting
salt and freshly ground black pepper

FOR THE FILLING
250 ml/1 cup white wine
1 carrot, roughly chopped
1 onion, roughly chopped
2 bay leaves
2 skinless chicken breasts, cut into 3-cm/1¼-inch pieces
1 large leek, sliced
50 g/3½ tablespoons butter, plus extra for mashing
1 tablespoon cornflour/cornstarch
1 heaped tablespoon wholegrain mustard
125 ml/½ cup double/heavy cream

FOR THE WINE SAUCE
500 ml/2 cups of the reserved chicken stock
200 ml/scant 1 cup double/heavy cream
1 teaspoon wholegrain mustard
1 tablespoon cornflour/cornstarch
15 g/1 tablespoon butter

Serves 4

Preheat the oven to 200°C (400°F) Gas 6.

Prick the skin of the potatoes and rub with salt. Bake in the preheated oven for 1 hour, or until tender. Alternatively, cook in the microwave for about 8 minutes, or until tender.

Pour the wine into a pan with 1 litre/4 cups of water and add the carrot, onion and bay leaves. Bring the liquid to the boil. Add the chicken to the pan and simmer for a few minutes, then remove from the heat and leave for 20 minutes. Check that the chicken is cooked, then strain the poaching liquid and reserve to use later.

In a large frying pan/skillet, fry the leek in the butter, season and cook until soft. Add the cornflour to the pan and stir then add the chicken and mustard. Add the cream and 100 ml/scant ½ cup of the reserved chicken stock simmer for a few minutes until the sauce starts to thicken. Remove from the heat and let cool.

Cut a small hole in the top of each cooled potato. Scoop out the flesh but leave a layer of potato around the edge of the skin. Place the scooped-out potato into a bowl, mash with butter and season to taste. Spoon the chicken mixture into the cavity of each potato so that it is a little higher than the top of the potato.

Preheat the oven to 180°C (350°F) Gas 4.

On a flour-dusted surface, roll out the pastry to 5 mm/¼ inch thick. Cut rounds 1–2 cm/½–¾ inch larger than the opening on the top of each potato. Brush beaten egg over one side of the pastry. Place the pastry over the potato, egg-side down, and use a fork to crimp the edges. Brush the top of the pastry with egg and cut a small hole in the top of each pie. Place on a baking sheet and bake in the oven for 25–30 minutes until the pastry is golden.

For the sauce, put the reserved chicken stock in a pan with any leftover filling and simmer until the liquid has reduced by half. Add the cream and mustard. Rub the cornflour into the butter and add to the pan, then simmer until the sauce thickens. Strain and serve warm with the pies and mash.

This recipe makes the perfect use of a jacket potato. Potato skins hollowed and filled with fish in a cheesy white sauce with the potato piped into a classic pie topping. Markets often sell packs of fish pie mix with a selection of fresh fish pieces, making this comforting dish easy to prepare.

Fish pie jacket

4 large baking potatoes
2 tablespoons milk
30 g/2 tablespoons butter
300 g/10½ oz. fresh fish pieces such as salmon, haddock, cod and raw peeled shrimp/prawns
100 g/¾ cup frozen peas
1 tablespoon chopped fresh parsley
salt and freshly ground black pepper

FOR THE CHEESE SAUCE
30 g/2 tablespoons butter
2 tablespoons plain/all-purpose flour
400 ml/1¾ cups milk
120 g/⅓ cups grated Cheddar, plus extra for sprinkling
1 teaspoon wholegrain mustard

piping/pastry bag with large star nozzle/tip

Serves 4

Preheat the oven to 200°C (400°F) Gas 6.

Prick the skin of the potatoes and rub with salt. Bake in the preheated oven for 1 hour, or until tender. Alternatively, cook in the microwave for about 8 minutes, or until tender.

Cut off the tops of the potatoes and scoop out the flesh into a mixing bowl. Leave enough potato around the edge of the skins so that they hold their shape and will be a stable bowl to contain the fish pie filling. Add the milk and butter to the potato and mash until smooth. Season with salt and pepper. Spoon the potato into the piping bag and set aside.

Whilst the potatoes are cooking, prepare the cheese sauce. Heat the butter in a saucepan over a gentle heat until melted, then add the flour and whisk to incorporate into the butter. Cook for a few minutes over the heat, taking care that the flour mixture does not burn. Slowly whisk the milk in, a little at a time, so that lumps do not form. Add the grated cheese to the white sauce with the mustard and whisk over a gentle heat until the cheese has melted and the sauce has thickened. Season with salt and pepper.

Preheat the oven to 180°C (350°F) Gas 4.

Add the fish and peas to the cheese sauce and spoon into the potato skins. Pipe the potato on top to cover the fish pie filling. If you do not have a piping bag, spoon the potato on top and make soft peaks or patterns with a fork. Sprinkle with extra grated cheese.

Place on a greased baking sheet and bake in the preheated oven for 20–25 minutes until the tops of the potatoes are golden brown. Sprinkle with the chopped parsley, and serve.

Haggis – the national dish of Scotland – is somewhat of an acquired taste, but paired with a whisky sauce, it makes a rich and tasty supper on a steaming jacket potato. Haggis is traditionally served with Neaps and Tatties (turnips and potatoes) which makes a jacket potato the perfect accompaniment for haggis.

Jacket with haggis & whisky sauce

4 large baking potatoes
400 g/14 oz. haggis

FOR THE WHISKY SAUCE
1 large onion, finely chopped
15 g/1 tablespoon butter
3 tablespoons whisky
125 ml/½ cup vegetable stock
1 teaspoon wholegrain mustard
125 ml/½ cup double/heavy cream
salt and freshly ground black pepper

FOR THE BACON LATTICE
8 rashers/slices smoked streaky/fatty bacon
24 fresh chives

Serves 4

Preheat the oven to 200°C (400°F) Gas 6.

Prick the skin of the potatoes and rub with salt. Bake in the preheated oven for 1 hour, or until tender. Alternatively, cook in the microwave for about 8 minutes, or until tender.

Cook the haggis following the packet instructions and keep warm until you are ready to serve.

For the sauce, in a frying pan/skillet, cook the chopped onion in the butter until it is soft and starts to caramelize. If the onion starts to stick or burn, add a little water to the pan. When the onion is soft, pour the whisky into the pan and cook for a few minutes. Add the stock and cook down until the stock has reduced by half. Add the mustard and cream and simmer over a gentle heat until the sauce thickens. Season with salt and pepper and keep warm.

Preheat the grill/broiler to high.

To make the bacon lattices, cut the bacon into thin strips about 10 cm/4 inches in length so that you have eight for each lattice. Weave the bacon strips and chives on a sheet of foil on a baking sheet to make four lattices. Grill/broil for 3–5 minutes, turning halfway through cooking, until the bacon is cooked.

To serve, cut the potatoes open and top each with a slices of the haggis. Pour over the whisky sauce and top each with a bacon lattice. Serve straight away.

FIRESIDE SNACKS & SUPPERS

Baked eggs are the perfect Sunday night supper in winter, when you've had a big lunch and just want something comforting but simple to eat in front of the TV. The fillings can be determined by what you have in the fridge. It might be leftover roast items, a curry, stir-fried greens, a beef chilli/chili... there are so many options. You generally add the fillings first and then the egg, but add lighter things like cheese, cream or herbs on top. Have a go and see which way you like best.

Baked eggs

2 teaspoons butter, at room temperature
4–5 tablespoons filling per egg (see below for some ideas)
4 eggs
4 tablespoons single/light cream
salt and freshly ground black pepper
toast, to serve

4 ramekins or a couple of shallow ovenproof dishes, depending on whether you want individual baked eggs or a sharing set-up

Serves 2

Preheat the oven to 250°C (475°F) Gas 9.

Grease the ramekins or dishes with the butter, then fill with your chosen fillings. Break an egg into each ramekin (or 2 eggs per dish) over the top of the fillings, then pour over a splash of cream and a sprinkle of seasoning.

Place the ramekins or dishes on a baking sheet and bake in the preheated oven for 10–14 minutes until cooked through but softly set. If it's a thicker ramekin or you've chosen a larger dish with multiple eggs inside, the eggs may need a little longer in the oven (this is because cold fillings in the ramekins absorb some of that heat, so after 10 minutes, keep a close eye on them but remember that they'll continue to cook slightly once out the oven). Serve with toast.

FILLING IDEAS
Leftover roast veg, ragù, cooked meat, baked beans, meaty curry, dahl, pasta sauce, fresh leafy greens, smoked salmon, sliced mushrooms, fresh spinach, cheese... the list goes on!

FIRESIDE SNACKS & SUPPERS

In place of milk, beer is used to bind the batter for these hearty pancakes. It gives the pancakes a savoury, malty flavour, and with the addition of salty bacon and sweet maple syrup, they really are the perfect sweet and savoury combination.

Beer & bacon pancakes

200 g/7 oz. smoked bacon lardons
12 rashers/slices of smoked streaky/fatty bacon
160 g/1⅓ cups self-raising/self-rising flour, sifted
1 teaspoon baking powder
1 egg, separated
60 g/⅓ cup dark brown soft sugar
a pinch of salt
250 ml/1 cup beer
3 tablespoons melted butter, plus extra for frying
maple syrup, to serve

Serves 2

Begin by frying all of the bacon in a dry frying pan/skillet – they will release sufficient oil as you cook them to prevent them sticking so you do not need to add any extra fat to the pan. Remove from the pan and put on a paper towel to remove any excess fat. Set aside while you prepare the batter.

To make the pancake batter, put the flour, baking powder, egg yolk, dark brown sugar, salt and beer in a large mixing bowl and whisk together. Add in the melted butter and cooked bacon lardons and whisk again. The batter should have a smooth, dropping consistency.

In a separate bowl, whisk the egg white to stiff peaks. Gently fold the whisked egg white into the batter mixture using a spatula. Cover and put in the refrigerator to rest for 30 minutes.

When you are ready to serve, remove your batter mixture from the refrigerator and stir gently. Put a little butter in a large frying pan set over a medium heat. Allow the butter to melt and coat the base of the pan, then ladle small amounts of the rested batter into the pan, leaving a little space between each. Cook until the underside of each pancake is golden brown and a few bubbles start to appear on the top – this will take 2–3 minutes. Turn the pancake over using a spatula and cook on the other side until golden.

Serve the pancakes with the streaky bacon and lashings of maple syrup.

This is an all-time family favourite that doesn't take long to make and that everyone loves. You can buy sausagemeat in most supermarkets or you can make your own with minced/ground pork and bacon. Or, if pushed for time, use your favourite butcher's sausages and squeeze them out of their skins. The lattice is easy to make once you get the hang of it. There are gadgets called lattice rollers, but these are too fiddly and delicate for this. Serve with baked beans for the ultimate comfort food!

Simple sausage lattice slice

2 tablespoons lard or vegetable oil
1 small onion, finely chopped
400 g/14 oz. good sausagemeat (or your favourite sausages squeezed out of their skins)
1 teaspoon dried mixed herbs
2 tablespoons mango chutney
1 tablespoon Dijon mustard
1 teaspoon garlic salt (optional)
1 sheet of ready-rolled shortcrust pastry
1 egg, beaten
salt and freshly ground black pepper

Serves 4

Preheat the oven to 200°C (400°F) Gas 6.

Melt the lard or heat the oil in a large saucepan set over a medium heat, add the onion and fry until it is soft and translucent. Transfer to a large mixing bowl and add the sausagemeat, herbs, chutney, mustard, garlic salt (if using) and plenty of pepper. Using your hands or a wooden spoon, work it all together until evenly mixed.

Unroll the pastry, cut out a 32-cm/13-inch square and slide it onto a baking sheet.

Shape the sausagemeat into a log about 7.5 cm/3 inches wide and lay it in the centre of the pastry, leaving a 2-fingers'-width margin at either end. Make 7–8 evenly spaced diagonal cuts in the pastry along the two long sides on either side of the sausagemeat filling.

Dampen the edges of the pastry with a little water. Fold each unslashed pastry edge over the ends of the sausagemeat, and then fold over the long sides, overlapping the cut pieces to give a plaited/braided effect. Brush the slice with the beaten egg for a shiny glaze. Sprinkle over a pinch of salt.

Bake in the preheated oven for about 40 minutes until the pastry is crisp and golden, and the sausagemeat is cooked right through. Slice and serve hot.

Everyone just loves sausage rolls, especially served warm straight out of the oven – but they also make a fantastic gourmet lunchbox treat. If fresh chorizo sausage is difficult to find, use a good garlicky butcher's sausage and mix in 1–2 teaspoons of sweet or hot Spanish pimentón (smoked paprika) and a couple of tablespoons of red wine.

Chorizo & black olive sausage rolls

400 g/14 oz. fresh cooking chorizo sausages (not the harder salami type)

2 tablespoons chopped fresh parsley or coriander/cilantro

25 g/3 tablespoons very finely chopped red onion or shallot

2 tablespoons roughly chopped black olives

1 sheet of ready-rolled shortcrust pastry

1 egg, beaten

a little warm milk mixed with a pinch of powdered saffron

salt and freshly ground black pepper

Makes 12

Preheat the oven to 200°C (400°F) Gas 6 and line a baking sheet with baking paper.

Squeeze the chorizo sausages out of their skins and into a large mixing bowl. Add the parsley, red onion and olives and season with salt and pepper. Using your hands, mix and squeeze the mixture until well combined.

Unroll the pastry and cut in half lengthways to make two rectangles. With floured hands, roll the meat mixture into two long sausages the same length as the pastry and place one down the centre of each piece.

Dampen the pastry along one long edge of each rectangle, then bring the dry pastry up and over the sausagemeat, followed by the dampened side, pressing the edges together. Flip each roll over, making sure that the join is underneath the roll.

Combine the beaten egg with the saffron-infused milk and brush over the rolls carefully, then cut into 5-cm/2-inch lengths. Either prick each one with a skewer a few times, or snip a couple of small 'V's in the pastry with a pair of scissors. (This allows steam to escape during cooking and stops the pastry from over-puffing up.) Arrange on the prepared baking sheet and bake in the preheated oven for 25–30 minutes until set and golden. Serve warm.

These pasties are almost like corned beef hash in pastry. Orange-fleshed sweet potatoes are used here, which have a lovely smooth texture and rich, sweet earthy taste, and contrast nicely with the saltiness of the corned beef. The fresh thyme is essential, and lemon thyme is even better.

Corned beef & sweet potato pasties

2 sheets of ready-rolled shortcrust pastry
2 tablespoons sunflower oil
1 onion, finely chopped
1 large orange-fleshed sweet potato, diced
2 tablespoons spicy mango chutney or sweet chilli/chili sauce
2 tablespoons chopped fresh thyme or lemon thyme
450 g/1 lb. canned corned beef, chilled and diced
1 egg, beaten
salt and freshly ground black pepper

Makes 6 large pasties or 12 smaller ones

Unroll the pastry and cut out six rounds, using a 20-cm/8-inch plate as a guide.

Heat the oil in a sauté pan and add the onion. Cook over medium heat for 5 minutes until beginning to soften. Add the sweet potato and cook, stirring from time to time, for 10 minutes, or until just tender. Stir in the chutney and thyme and leave to cool. Once cold, fold in the corned beef and season well.

Divide the mixture among the six pastry circles and crimp the edges together to seal in the filling – over the top or to the side, the choice is yours! Brush with the beaten egg and chill for 30 minutes.

Preheat the oven to 200°C (400°F) Gas 6 and line a baking sheet with baking paper.

Arrange the chilled pasties on the prepared baking sheet, make a little steam hole in each one and bake in the preheated oven for 20–30 minutes until the pastry is golden brown. Remove from the oven and serve hot or transfer to a wire rack to cool.

FOR THE PASTRY

150 g/1 cup plus 3 tablespoons spelt flour, plus extra for dusting
75 g/5 tablespoons butter, cubed
2 tablespoons cold water

FOR THE FILLING

1 tablespoon olive oil
1 shallot, chopped
300 g/10½ oz. white/cup mushrooms, sliced 1-cm/½-inch thick
300 g/1¼ cups double/heavy cream
2 eggs, plus 1 egg yolk
freshly grated nutmeg
100 g/3½ oz. blue cheese, crumbled into small chunks
50 g/⅓ cup walnut pieces
salt and freshly ground black pepper

24-cm/9½-inch loose-based fluted tart pan, lightly greased

baking beans

Makes 1 quiche

Mushroom quiche is a much-loved classic. In this version, a nutty tasting spelt flour crust encases a rich filling made from fried mushrooms and shallots, combined with savoury blue cheese. The bold earthy flavours make this a comforting winter dish.

Mushroom, blue cheese & walnut quiche

For the pastry, place the flour, a pinch of salt and the butter in a food processor. Pulse until the butter has been absorbed by the flour. Add the cold water and blend until the mixture forms a dough. Wrap the pastry in cling film/plastic wrap and chill in the fridge for 30 minutes.

For the filling, heat the olive oil in a frying pan/skillet. Fry the shallot over a medium heat for 2 minutes until softened. Add the mushrooms and fry over a high heat until lightly browned. Drain any liquid in a colander and allow to cool.

Preheat the oven to 200°C (400°F) Gas 6.

Roll out the pastry on a lightly floured work surface. Line the greased pan with the pastry, pressing it in firmly. Prick the base several times with a fork. Line the case with baking parchment and fill with baking beans. Blind bake the pastry case in the preheated oven for 15 minutes. Carefully remove the parchment and beans and bake for a further 5 minutes, then remove from the oven. Leave the oven on.

Meanwhile, whisk together the cream, eggs and egg yolk. Season with salt, black pepper and grated nutmeg. Sprinkle the blue cheese and walnuts in an even layer inside the pastry case. Top with the fried mushrooms and pour over the cream mixture. Bake for 40 minutes. Leave to cool slightly, and serve warm or at room temperature.

A poem of Calabrian flavours on a pizza! Try tracking down rapini to use instead of broccoli, known for its earthy, slightly bitter taste and beloved by Italian cooks. Increase the pizza dough quantities to make more pizzas.

'Nduja, broccoli, black olive & egg pizza

50 g/2 oz. purple sprouting broccoli or other broccoli, sliced in half lengthways

100 g/3½ oz. 'nduja (spicy Calabrian sausage)

1 teaspoon dried oregano

5–7 wrinkly pitted black olives

1 egg

extra virgin olive oil, to drizzle

salt and freshly ground black pepper

FOR THE PIZZA DOUGH

250 g/2 cups '00' flour, plus extra for dusting

½ teaspoon fine salt

1 teaspoon fast-action dried yeast

¼ teaspoon sugar

125 ml/½ cup hand-hot water

½ tablespoon olive oil

FOR THE PIZZAIOLA SAUCE

4 tablespoons olive oil

1 garlic clove, chopped

½ teaspoon dried oregano

400-g/14-oz. can chopped tomatoes

a testo, terracotta bakestone or a large, heavy baking sheet

a pizza peel or rimless baking sheet

Makes 1 medium-crust pizza (25–35 cm/10–14 inches)

To make the dough, sift the flour and salt into a large bowl and add the yeast and sugar. Make a well in the centre and add the water, followed by the olive oil. Bring the mixture together with your hands, then turn out onto a flour-dusted surface and knead for 5–10 minutes until smooth. Place into an oiled bowl, cover and leave to rise until doubled in size; about 1½ hours.

Once risen, punch out the air, roll into a smooth ball, cover and leave to rise again for 1–1½ hours.

For the sauce, heat the oil in a large shallow pan and add the garlic, oregano and tomatoes. Cook over a high heat for 5–8 minutes until thick and glossy. Pass through a food mill.

Put the testo, terracotta bakestone or a large, heavy baking sheet on the lower shelf of the oven. Preheat the oven to 220°C (425°F) Gas 7 for at least 30 minutes.

Blanche the broccoli in boiling salted water for 30 seconds, then drain and refresh in cold water.

Uncover the dough, punch out the air and roll or pull into a 25-cm/10-inch circle directly onto baking paper. Slide this onto the pizza peel or rimless baking sheet. Spread about 3–4 tablespoons pizzaiola sauce over the base, leaving a 1-cm/⅜-inch rim around the edge. Spoon over the 'nduja. Drain the broccoli and scatter over the pizza. Sprinkle with the dried oregano and olives, drizzle with olive oil, then season.

Working quickly, slide both paper and pizza onto the hot bakestone or baking sheet. Bake for 5 minutes, then slide out the baking parchment. Bake the pizza for a further 10 minutes, then break the egg into the middle (if using) and bake for 5 minutes, or until the egg is just cooked and the crust is golden. Remove from the oven and drizzle with olive oil.

This is a ridiculously indulgent winter warmer oozing melted cheese. You can sprinkle rinsed salted capers over the cheese to cut through the richness of it, if you like. You will have enough onion marmellata to use for other things – it's delicious with salty cheeses for example.

Burrata, potato, sage & red onion marmellata pizza pie

400 g/14 oz. potatoes
1 quantity Pizza Dough (see page 87)
250 g/9 oz. burrata cheese
2–3 sprigs of fresh sage or rosemary, broken into small pieces
bitter radicchio/Italian chicory and rocket/arugula salad, to serve

FOR THE RED ONION MARMELLATA
(MAKES ABOUT 500 G/18 OZ.)
800 g/1¾ lbs. red onions, thinly sliced
75 g/½ cup sultanas/golden raisins
150 g/¾ cup light soft brown sugar
75 g/⅓ cup golden caster/granulated sugar
50 ml/3½ tablespoons red wine
50 ml/3½ tablespoons red wine vinegar
2 teaspoons chopped fresh thyme
2 whole cloves
salt and freshly ground black pepper

a pizza pan or springform cake pan, 25 cm/10 inches diameter and 4 cm/1¾ inches deep, lightly oiled

Makes 1 pie (25 cm/10 inches)

First make the red onion marmellata. Put the sliced onions in a heavy casserole dish. Add the sultanas, sugars, wine, vinegar, thyme and cloves, season with salt and pepper, stir well, cover and leave to marinate for at least 2 hours or overnight. Cook over a medium heat for about 1 hour, stirring every now and then to prevent it catching. Watch carefully during the last 15 minutes of cooking that it doesn't catch and burn. It is ready when thick and there is no more liquid. Spoon into a screw-top jar with a layer of olive oil on top to exclude the air. This will keep for 3 months in a cool place.

Preheat the oven to 200°C (400°F) Gas 6 and put a baking sheet in the middle of the oven.

Meanwhile, put the potatoes in a pan of salted water and bring to the boil. Cook for 10 minutes, or until tender. Drain, then slice thickly.

Uncover the dough, punch out the air and roll into a rough 35-cm/14-inch circle. Use this to line the prepared pizza pan, draping extra dough over the edge if necessary. Scatter half the burrata over the base, followed by blobs of onion marmellata, the sliced potatoes and finally the remaining cheese. Sprinkle with rosemary or sage. Trim around the edge with a sharp knife and discard the excess dough.

Slide into the oven on top of the baking sheet and bake for 25–35 minutes until bubbling with a golden crust.

Remove from the oven and leave to stand for 10 minutes before serving in thick wedges.

These paprika mushrooms are inspired by German markets, served steaming in the chilly open-air festive markets. They are delicious on their own, but piled high on a jacket potato, this becomes a hearty dish that will bring a bit of warmth to any winter's evening.

Creamy paprika mushrooms

2 baking potatoes
15 g/1 tablespoon butter
300 g/10½ oz. button mushrooms, halved
1 teaspoon smoked paprika, sweet or hot
1 tablespoon brandy
1 teaspoon chopped fresh parsley
1 teaspoon thyme leaves
150 ml/⅔ cup soured/sour cream
squeeze of lemon juice, to taste
salt and freshly ground black pepper
snipped fresh chives, to garnish

Serves 2

Preheat the oven to 200°C (400°F) Gas 6.

Prick the skin of the potatoes and rub with salt. Bake in the preheated oven for 1 hour, or until tender. Alternatively, cook in the microwave for about 8 minutes, or until tender.

Whilst the potatoes are cooking, melt the butter in a pan, add the mushrooms and cook for 5–10 minutes until softened. Add the paprika to the pan with the brandy, parsley and thyme and cook for a few minutes further. Stir in the soured cream and reduce the heat to a very low setting. Season with lemon juice and salt and pepper. If the sauce splits, do not worry, just add a little more soured cream and it should recover.

Cut the potatoes open and top with the mushrooms, then garnish with fresh chives. Serve straight away.

FIRESIDE SNACKS & SUPPERS

It may sound weird to add Marmite to noodles and tofu, but it's really delicious and not overpowering. Marmite adds some umami or savoury depth without any effort at all. Even if you don't like Marmite, you will still enjoy this recipe.

Tofu noodles with mushrooms & marmite

rapeseed/canola oil, for frying
225 g/8 oz. smoked tofu, cut into 2-cm/¾-inch cubes
3 garlic cloves, thinly sliced
30-g/1-oz. piece of ginger, peeled and cut into matchsticks
1 red chilli/chile, thinly sliced
200 g/7 oz. mushrooms, thickly sliced
100 g/3½ oz. greens, sliced
2 tablespoons sesame oil
1 tablespoon Marmite/yeast extract
1 tablespoon rice vinegar
300 g/10½ oz. udon noodles
1 lime, cut into wedges
salt and freshly ground black pepper

Serves 2

Add a glug of rapeseed oil to large frying pan/skillet set over a medium–high heat and once hot, add the tofu cubes and fry them for about 10 minutes until golden on all sides, turning often. Transfer the golden tofu to a plate.

Pile the garlic, ginger, chilli and mushrooms into the pan. Fry for 5 minutes until softening and slightly browned. Add the greens and toss to combine, letting them wilt and briefly cook for 2 minutes.

Return the tofu to the pan and add the sesame oil, Marmite and vinegar. Stir to mix all the ingredients together, then push them to the sides of the pan to create a gap in the centre. Tip the noodles into the gap so they have direct contact with the base of the pan. Leave for 30 seconds, then start to jiggle them a bit to help them loosen up.

Toss all the ingredients together for a couple of minutes until piping hot and fully combined. Finish with a good squeeze of lime juice, then season and remove from the heat. Serve immediately.

This simple recipe makes a creamy macaroni and cheese that can be used as a base for further experimentation. Combining two mild cheeses, such as Cheddar and Monterey Jack, gives this dish a delicious yet delicate depth of flavour.

Classic mac 'n' cheese

500 g/1 lb. 2oz. macaroni
50 g/1 cup fresh breadcrumbs
salt and freshly ground black pepper

FOR THE BÉCHAMEL SAUCE
50 g/3½ tablespoons unsalted butter
60 g/6 tablespoons plain/all-purpose flour
625 ml/2½ cups milk
150 g/1¼ cups grated Monterey Jack or other mild, semi-hard cheese
150 g/1¾ cups grated medium Cheddar

Serves 6–8

Bring a large saucepan of salted water to the boil. Add the macaroni, stir well and cook according to the package instructions until very tender. Stir periodically to prevent the macaroni from sticking together. When cooked, drain, rinse well under running water and let drip dry in a colander.

Preheat the grill/broiler to medium.

To make the béchamel sauce, melt the butter in a saucepan. Stir in the flour and cook, stirring constantly, for 1 minute. Pour in the milk in a steady stream, whisking constantly, and continue to whisk for 3–5 minutes until the sauce begins to thicken. Season with plenty of salt. Remove from the heat and add the cheeses, mixing well with a spoon to incorporate. Taste and adjust the seasoning.

Put the cooked macaroni in a large mixing bowl. Pour over the hot béchamel sauce and mix well. Season to taste.

Transfer the macaroni mixture to a baking dish and spread evenly. Top with a good grinding of black pepper and sprinkle the breadcrumbs evenly over the top. Grill/broil for 5–10 minutes until the top is crunchy and golden brown, then serve immediately.

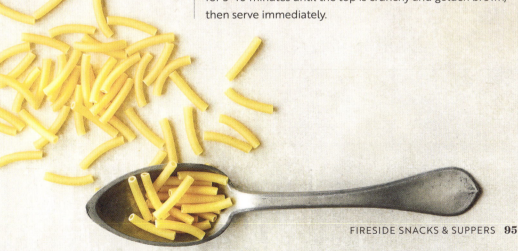

FIRESIDE SNACKS & SUPPERS

This is a superfast mid-week meal – and gnocchi makes a nice change from pasta. It uses a can of broccoli and Stilton soup to make the sauce, making it really quick to prepare. Serve with a tomato and red onion salad, if you want to add a bit of colour and freshness, too.

Oven-baked broccoli & blue cheese gnocchi

1 tablespoon olive oil
1 onion, finely chopped
1 garlic clove, chopped
1 small head broccoli, chopped
800 g/1¾ lb. ready-made gnocchi
400-g/14-oz. can broccoli and Stilton soup
50 g/1¾ oz. cream cheese
salt and freshly ground black pepper

Serves 4

Preheat the oven to 220°C (425°F) Gas 7.

Heat the olive oil in an ovenproof frying pan/skillet over a medium heat and fry the onion, garlic and broccoli for a few minutes. Add 250 ml/1 cup water, cover and leave to simmer for 6 minutes until the broccoli is cooked and tender.

Remove the lid and add the gnocchi. Pour in the soup, season generously and stir to mix everything together. Bring to a simmer and, once simmering, remove from the heat, stir in the cream cheese and place the pan in the oven for 12–15 minutes, or until the gnocchi is soft and cooked.

Serve with a tomato and red onion salad on the side (if liked) and some crusty bread for mopping up the cheesy sauce.

Note *If you've got any small bits of leftover blue cheese like Stilton lurking in the fridge you can crumble that in instead of adding the cream cheese, it will give it a stronger flavour.*

A strongly flavoured cheese such as Gorgonzola pairs beautifully with a cream sauce here. Smoky pancetta and a tomato reduction both have equally punchy flavours that match up to the pungent cheese well.

500 g/1 lb. 2 oz. macaroni
2 tablespoons olive oil
1 onion, finely chopped
200 g/7 oz. pancetta, chopped
½ teaspoon dried thyme
1 x 400-g/14-oz. can chopped tomatoes
pinch of sugar
600 ml/2½ cups double/heavy cream
200 g/1½ cups crumbled Gorgonzola
50 g/⅔ cups grated Parmesan
50 g/1 cup fresh breadcrumbs
salt and freshly ground black pepper

Serves 6–8

Pancetta, gorgonzola & tomato mac 'n' cheese

Bring a large saucepan of salted water to the boil. Add the macaroni, stir well and cook according to the package instructions until very tender. Stir periodically to prevent the macaroni from sticking together. When cooked, drain, rinse well under running water and let drip dry in a colander.

Heat the oil in a large frying pan/skillet. Add the onion and cook over a high heat for about 5 minutes until just caramelized, stirring occasionally. Stir in the pancetta and thyme, and cook for 2–3 minutes until browned, stirring occasionally. Add the tomatoes, sugar and 1 teaspoon of salt and simmer very gently for 15–30 minutes until the mixture has reduced to a jam-like consistency. Transfer to a large bowl and set aside.

Preheat the grill/broiler to medium–high.

Put the cream in a large saucepan and bring just to the boil, then reduce the heat. Add the cheeses and stir well to melt.

Put the cooked macaroni in the bowl with the tomato mixture. Pour over the hot cream sauce and mix well. Taste and adjust the seasoning.

Transfer the macaroni mixture to a baking dish and spread evenly. Top with a good grinding of black pepper and sprinkle the breadcrumbs evenly over the top. Grill/broil for 5–10 minutes until the top is crunchy and golden brown. Serve immediately.

This pasta bake is a lovely, wholesome veggie alternative to a traditional meat lasagne – and it equally hits the spot. You could try it with other vegetables, but this combination is a real winner.

Butternut squash & chicory pasta bake

800–900 g/1¾–2 lb. butternut squash
olive oil, for roasting
50 g/3½ tablespoons butter
50 g/6 tablespoons plain/
    all-purpose flour
650 ml/2¾ cups whole milk
40 g/½ cup grated Parmesan,
    plus extra to top
2 heads chicory
8–10 dried lasagne sheets
250 g/1¼ cups ricotta
20 g/1 oz. fresh basil
salt and freshly ground black pepper

Serves 6

Preheat the oven to 220°C (425°F) Gas 7.

Trim, then chop the butternut squash into 2.5-cm/1-inch chunks (no need to peel). Add to a large baking sheet, season well, drizzle with a glug of olive oil and toss to coat. Place on the top shelf of the oven and roast for 35 minutes until tender and lightly caramelized.

Melt the butter in a medium saucepan set over a medium heat and, once sizzling, add the flour. Mix very well and cook for a couple minutes. Next, add a splash of milk, which will turn the roux firmer. Allow the milk to be absorbed before you add another generous splash. Continue this process until all the milk is used. Let the sauce cook and thicken for about 5 minutes, stirring constantly – it should end up with a custard-like thickness. Remove from the heat, add the Parmesan, stir to combine, then season very well (make sure you taste it).

Separate the chicory leaves, then cut them in half lengthways. Scatter a layer of squash on the base of a baking dish, followed by chicory, some dollops of ricotta randomly placed, then a layer of lasagne sheets. Top with the white sauce and a scattering of basil leaves (and their stalks, torn). Repeat the layers (starting with the roasted squash), continuing until you've used up all of the ingredients. Finish with a very generous scattering of basil leaves on the final layer of béchamel and an extra sprinkle of seasoning and Parmesan, too.

Place on the middle shelf of the oven and bake for 40 minutes until tender, golden brown on top and bubbling.

It is the strong aroma and fruity tang of Taleggio in this recipe that transforms it from an ordinary mushroom and cheese dish into something truly sublime. Be sure to use fresh tarragon if you can find it.

Mushroom, tarragon & Taleggio pasta bake

500 g/1 lb. 2 oz. short pasta
300 g/10½ oz. Portobello mushrooms, stems trimmed level with cap
2–3 tablespoons vegetable oil
leaves from a few sprigs of fresh parsley, finely chopped
leaves from a few sprigs of fresh tarragon, finely chopped
600 ml/2½ cups double/heavy cream
100 g/generous 1 cup grated Cheddar
50 g/⅔ cup grated Parmesan
250 g/9 oz. Taleggio, thinly sliced
salt and freshly ground black pepper

Serves 6–8

Bring a large saucepan of salted water to the boil. Add the pasta, stir well and cook according to the package instructions until very tender. Stir periodically to prevent the pasta from sticking together. When cooked, drain, rinse well under running water and let drip dry in a colander.

Preheat the oven to 200°C (400°F) Gas 6.

Arrange the mushrooms in a single layer on a baking sheet, stems up, and brush with the oil. Season lightly with salt, sprinkle over the herbs and roast in the preheated oven for 15–20 minutes until tender. Remove and let cool slightly. Slice the mushrooms and set aside.

Preheat the grill/broiler to medium.

Put the cream in a large saucepan and bring just to the boil, stirring occasionally, then reduce the heat. Add the Cheddar and Parmesan and half the Taleggio, and stir well to melt. Taste and adjust the seasoning.

Put the cooked pasta in a large mixing bowl. Stir in half the sliced mushrooms, pour over the hot cream sauce and mix well. Taste and adjust the seasoning. Transfer the pasta mixture to a baking dish and spread evenly. Top with the remaining mushrooms and Taleggio slices and a good grinding of black pepper.

Grill/broil for 5–10 minutes until the top is golden and serve immediately.

Cottage pie goes upmarket! Using a touch of truffle oil to flavour the mashed potato is a simple but effective way to give a new dimension to this homely dish. Adding mushrooms to the meat mixture brings texture as well as flavour. Bake until golden brown and serve it straight from the oven, accompanied by veggies, for a soul-soothing meal.

Truffled mash cottage pie

1 tablespoon vegetable oil
1 bay leaf
1 onion, finely chopped
1 celery stick, finely chopped
½ carrot, peeled and finely chopped
500 g/1 lb. 2 oz. lean minced/ground beef
150 g/5 oz. white/cup and button mushrooms, chopped
a splash of dry white wine (optional)
3 tablespoons tomato purée/paste
100 ml/scant ½ cup beef or chicken stock
900 g/2 lb. fluffy/Idaho potatoes, peeled and cut into chunks
2 teaspoons butter
2 tablespoons double/heavy cream
½ teaspoon truffle oil
3 tablespoons grated Cheddar
1 tablespoon grated Parmesan
salt and freshly ground black pepper

Serves 4

Preheat the oven to 200°C (400°F) Gas 6.

Heat the oil in a large frying pan/skillet over a medium heat. Add the bay leaf, onion, celery and carrot and fry, stirring, until the onion is softened. Add the beef and fry until browned, stirring often.

Add the mushrooms and fry for 3 minutes. Pour in the white wine (if using) and fry briefly until cooked off. Mix in the tomato purée and the stock. Season with salt and black pepper. Simmer for 10–15 minutes, stirring often.

Meanwhile, cook the potatoes in a large pan of salted, boiling water until tender; about 20 minutes. Drain, then mash with butter, cream and truffle oil and season with salt and black pepper.

Place the beef mixture in an ovenproof dish. Top with the mashed potato, spreading it in an even layer. Sprinkle over the Cheddar and Parmesan cheese.

Bake in the preheated oven for 30 minutes until golden brown. Serve hot from the oven.

A homely recipe, which everyone will enjoy. The crisp, buttery pastry contrasts nicely with the soft, cheesy potato filling. Serve with green vegetables to cut through the richness of the cheese.

Potato & cheese pie

FOR THE PASTRY

225 g/1¾ cups plain/all-purpose flour, plus extra for dusting
pinch of salt
125 g/9 tablespoons butter, cubed
2–3 tablespoons cold water

FOR THE FILLING

400 g/14 oz. potatoes, peeled and cut into chunks
2 onions, quartered and thinly sliced
1 tablespoon vegetable or sunflower oil
25 g/1½ tablespoons butter
freshly grated nutmeg
100 g/1 cup plus 2 tablespoons grated Cheddar cheese
2 tablespoons chopped fresh parsley
full-fat/whole milk, for brushing
salt and freshly ground black pepper

20-cm/8-inch deep, loose-based fluted tart pan, greased

Serves 4–6

First, make the pastry. Mix together the flour and salt, then rub in the butter with your fingertips until absorbed. Mix in the cold water until the mixture comes together to form a dough. Wrap in cling film/plastic wrap and chill in the fridge for 30 minutes.

For the filling, cook the potatoes in a large pan of boiling, salted water until tender; drain.

Meanwhile, gently fry the onions in the oil over a low heat, stirring often, for 10 minutes, until thoroughly softened.

Mash the cooked potatoes thoroughly with the butter. Season well with freshly grated nutmeg, salt and freshly ground black pepper. Stir in the Cheddar cheese, fried onions and parsley. Set aside to cool.

Preheat the oven to 200°C (400°F) Gas 6.

Roll out two-thirds of the pastry on a lightly floured work surface. Use the pastry to line the greased tart pan, pressing it in well. Fill the pastry case with the potato mixture.

Roll out the remaining pastry and cut out a pie lid. Brush the edges of the pie case with milk and top with the pie lid, pressing the edges together to seal. Brush the pastry lid with milk and cut three slashes in the centre of the pie.

Bake the pie in the preheated oven for 50 minutes until golden brown. Serve hot, warm or at room temperature.

FIRESIDE SNACKS & SUPPERS 107

SWEET THINGS

An elegant, grown-up cookie with the addition of dark rye flour and delicious studs of melting dark chocolate. Very moreish!

Chocolate chip rye cookies

120 g/9 tablespoons unsalted butter, softened
200 g/1 cup golden caster/granulated sugar
½ teaspoon baking powder
a pinch of salt
1 large/US extra-large egg
seeds of 1 vanilla pod/bean
160 g/1½ cups dark rye flour
180 g/generous 1 cup dark/bittersweet chocolate chips

Makes 16

In a stand mixer, cream the butter and sugar until light and fluffy. Add the baking powder and salt and mix for another minute. Add the egg and vanilla seeds and mix to combine. Add the rye flour and gently mix until a uniform dough forms, then mix in the chocolate chips until well distributed. Flatten the dough into a disc, cover with cling film/plastic wrap and refrigerate for at least 20 minutes.

When ready to bake, preheat the oven to 180°C (350°F) Gas 4. Line 2 baking sheets with baking paper.

Divide the dough into 16 portions, rolling each into a ball. Place on the lined baking sheets at least 7.5 cm/3 inches apart. Bake in the preheated oven for 16 minutes, turning the baking sheets halfway through for an even bake.

Allow to cool completely on a wire rack before serving. Store in an airtight container for up to 3 days.

These are really great, they're like a mini cheesecake but in biscuit form, with the most amazing filling. You can make both parts ahead of time.

Cinnamon & salted butter biscuits

FOR THE SALTED BUTTER CHEESECAKE FILLING

25 g/1¾ tablespoons unsalted butter

25 g/2 tablespoons dark brown soft sugar

75 ml/⅓ cup double/heavy cream

¼ teaspoon sea salt

100 g/scant ½ cup cream cheese

FOR THE SHORTBREAD BISCUITS

130 g/9 tablespoons salted butter, softened

50 g/heaping ⅓ cup icing/confectioner's sugar

½ teaspoon ground cinnamon

160 g/1½ cups plain/all-purpose flour

Makes 12

Make the salted butter sauce first as it needs a while to cool. Add the butter, sugar, cream and sea salt to a saucepan set over a low–medium heat and whisk continuously for about 3 minutes as the ingredients gently melt and meld into one another. Once all the sugar has dissolved and the ingredients have combined, bring the mixture up to the boil and let bubble very vigorously for 2 minutes. Remove from the heat and let the bubbles subside. Set aside and let the salted butter sauce cool.

To make the shortbread biscuits add the butter, sugar and cinnamon to a large mixing bowl, then briefly combine using an electric, hand-held whisk until well combined. Then add the flour until just combined and looking like chunky, fudgy breadcrumbs.

Tip the mix onto a clean work surface and bring together with your hands into a rough log about 6 cm/2½ inches in diameter. You can handle it a little, but don't 'knead'; the soft butter will help bring everything together easily and if you play with the dough too much, you'll end up with tough shortbread. Transfer the log onto a large piece of parchment paper (or cling film/plastic wrap) and roll into a tight log, tying up both ends to seal. Transfer the log to the freezer and let firm up for 20 minutes.

When ready to bake, preheat the oven to 200°C (400°F) Gas 6. Line a large baking sheet with baking paper.

Unwrap the log, and slice it into discs 5 mm/¼ inch thick – you should get about 24. Lay them out on the baking sheet, transfer straight to the top shelf of the preheated oven and bake for 12–15 minutes until cooked, sandy and slightly coloured at the edges. Place the baking sheet on a cooling rack and leave to cool.

Once the salted butter sauce has come down to room temperature, place the cream cheese in a mixing bowl and add 90 g/3 oz. of the sauce, mixing well to combine. Spread the filling onto the base of half the biscuits, then top them with another biscuit – like a Jammy Dodger or an Oreo! There you have it, they're ready.

Not many people can resist a freshly baked chewy chocolate packed cookie – it's a bit like trying to say no to still-warm, straight-from-the-oven baked bread. One whiff of the heavenly smell coming from the oven alone, and self-restraint goes out of the window. For the best cookie, use good-quality chocolate chips – a mixture of dark and milk chocolate is used here, but you can stick to all of one or the other if you prefer. Or, for nutty cookies, add a handful of halved, toasted hazelnuts and slightly less chocolate.

Classic choc chip cookies

175 g/1½ sticks butter, softened
80 g/scant ½ cup soft brown sugar
80 g/scant ½ cup caster/granulated sugar
1 egg
225 g/1¾ cups plain/all-purpose flour
½ teaspoon bicarbonate of soda/baking soda
100 g/⅔ cup milk/semi-sweet chocolate chips
100 g/⅔ cup dark/bittersweet chocolate chips

Makes about 25

Preheat the oven to 180°C (350°F) Gas 4 and line 2 baking sheets with baking paper.

Put the butter and sugars together in a large mixing bowl and beat until light and fluffy. Add the egg and stir until fully incorporated. Mix the flour and bicarbonate of soda/baking soda together in a separate bowl and stir this into the cookie mixture. Add the chocolate chips and work everything together until evenly combined.

Roll the mixture into walnut-sized balls and arrange on the baking sheets, leaving a little space for spreading between each one.

Bake in the preheated oven for 8–10 minutes, until golden and firm.

Leave to cool for 5 minutes or so on the baking sheets, then transfer to a wire rack to cool completely. Store in an airtight container or cookie jar and eat within 5 days.

These cookies are a doddle to make – and an absolute delight to eat. They contain orange-flavoured chocolate, but you could also add a tablespoon of orange liqueur, if you happen to have some in the cupboard. Perfect served with a luxurious hot chocolate on a chilly afternoon.

Chocolate orange pillows

200 g/7 oz. dark/bittersweet chocolate
200 g/7 oz. orange-flavoured chocolate
50 g/3½ tablespoons butter
3 eggs
100 g/⅔ cup ground almonds
100 g/¾ cup plain/all-purpose flour
100 g/1 cup icing/confectioners sugar
1 teaspoon baking powder
grated zest of 2 oranges

FOR THE COATING
50 g/½ cup icing/confectioners' sugar
50 g/¼ cup caster/granulated sugar

Makes 25-30

Preheat the oven to 180°C (350°F) Gas 4 and line 2 baking sheets with baking paper.

Melt all the chocolate and butter together in a large mixing bowl set over a saucepan of barely simmering water (or microwave on full power for a minute or so, stirring half way through). Leave to cool a little and then beat in the eggs.

Add the ground almonds, flour, icing sugar and baking powder and beat until well mixed. Add the orange zest and stir until evenly mixed. Pop the mixture in the fridge for 30 minutes or so to firm up.

Put the icing sugar and caster sugar for coating in separate wide, shallow dishes and set aside.

Form the dough into balls the size of walnuts, then roll each ball in the icing sugar, then in the caster sugar, and then back in the icing sugar again. Arrange the cookie balls on the prepared baking sheets, leaving a little space for spreading between each one.

Bake in the preheated oven for about 10 minutes until the cookies are firm on the outside but still soft in the centre.

Leave to cool slightly on the baking sheets, before transferring to a wire rack to cool completely. Store in an airtight container and eat within 3 days.

Take your brownies to the next level by upping your chocolate game to use something like this Valrhona's Ampamakia, which takes the humble brownie to new heights of gourmet indulgence!

Chocolate brownies

100 g/¾ cup plain/all-purpose flour, sifted
100 g/1 cup unsweetened cocoa powder
1 teaspoon fine sea salt
345 g/3 sticks unsalted butter, cut into cubes
3 large (US extra-large) eggs
350 g/1¾ cups caster/granulated sugar
½ teaspoon pure vanilla extract or vanilla bean paste
200 g/7 oz. Valrhona Ampamakia (64% or 70% according to your own taste) or other dark/bittersweet chocolate, chopped
icing/confectioners' sugar, for dusting (optional)

a 23-cm/9-in. square brownie pan, greased and floured

Makes 12

Preheat the oven to 175°C (350°F) Gas 4.

Sift the flour, cocoa powder and salt into a mixing bowl and set aside until needed.

Put half the butter cubes in a medium heatproof bowl and set aside.

Put the remaining butter cubes in a saucepan set over a medium heat and melt, stirring. Pour the melted butter over the cubed butter and stir to combine. The butter should look creamy, with bits of unmelted butter still present and floating.

Put the eggs, sugar and vanilla extract in a separate bowl and beat with a handheld electric whisk set to a medium speed for about 3 minutes until the mixture is light and doubled in volume.

Using a lower speed, alternate adding the flour and the butter in several additions. Stir in 175 g/6 oz. of the chopped chocolate, reserving the rest.

Pour the mixture into the prepared pan and scatter the reserved pieces of chocolate over the top. Bake in the preheated oven for 35–40 minutes until the surface looks firm but a skewer inserted in the centre comes out slightly sticky with mixture.

Let the brownie cool in the pan before cutting into 12 squares. Dust lightly with icing sugar (if using) just before serving.

SWEET THINGS

When made this way with little oil and no refined sugar, these individual strudels, packed with fruit and aromatic citrus juice, can be a surprisingly healthy vegan option for a warming winter dessert.

Individual pear strudels

500 g/1 lb. 2 oz. (10 large sheets) filo/phyllo pastry
15 dried apricots, chopped
2 tablespoons rum
2 teaspoons pure vanilla extract
freshly squeezed juice and grated zest of 2 lemons or oranges
a pinch of salt
8 ripe pears
85 g/⅓ cup apple juice concentrate or pure maple syrup
65 g/¼ cup coconut oil mixed with 4 tablespoons water

Makes 20 slices

Take the filo/phyllo sheets out of the fridge 30 minutes before making the strudel. This will prevent the sheets from cracking during baking.

Meanwhile, put the apricots in a bowl with the rum, vanilla extract, lemon juice and zest and allow to soak while you prepare the pears, or longer if possible.

Preheat the oven to 180°C (350°F) Gas 4 and grease a large baking pan.

Peel and core the pears. Cut them into small cubes and mix them with the soaked apricots and the apple concentrate or syrup. Divide the mixture into five equal portions.

Place a sheet of filo on a dry work surface with the longer side facing you. (Cover the remaining sheets with cling film/plastic wrap to prevent them from drying out.) Brush the coconut oil mixture lightly over the sheet. Cover it with another sheet (this one doesn't need oiling).

Spread one portion of pears lengthwise along the bottom edge of the sheet. Arrange them in a 6-cm/2½-inch-wide strip, leaving a 2-cm/¾-inch edge on each side to prevent the filling from spilling out. Roll the sheet up carefully around the filling and place in the greased baking pan. Repeat with the remaining sheets and filling to get five strudels in the pan. Brush them lightly with the coconut oil mixture and use a sharp knife to score each strudel into four slices.

Bake the strudels in the preheated oven for 25–30 minutes or until golden. Serve warm.

All you really need for a good frangipane is butter, sugar, eggs and ground almonds, though a small amount of flour helps give these upside-down puddings a bit more structural integrity. The hot puddings are delicious topped with a scoop of ice cream, which will melt like pooling snow over the pudding's craggy tops.

Apricot frangipane puddings

450 g/1 lb. apricot flesh
  (about 10 pitted fresh apricots)
50 g/¼ cup brown/muscovado sugar
110 g/1 stick unsalted butter,
  at room temperature
110 g/½ cup caster/granulated sugar
2 large (US extra-large) eggs, beaten
130 g/1⅓ cup ground almonds
3 tablespoons plain/all-purpose flour,
  plus extra for dusting
icing/confectioners' sugar, for dusting
ice cream, to serve (optional)

6 ramekins, greased and dusted
  with flour

Serves 6

Preheat the oven to 180°C (350°F) Gas 4.

Cut the apricots into quarters and simmer in a pan with the brown sugar and 1 tablespoon water for 3 minutes. Arrange the apricots over the bottom of the ramekins.

Cream the butter and caster sugar together until pale and fluffy, then beat in the eggs one at a time. Carefully fold in the almonds and flour, then spoon the mixture over the apricots.

Bake in the preheated oven for 30 minutes. Remove from the oven and leave to cool for 5 minutes, then turn out onto serving plates, ensuring all of the fruit tumbles out to sit on top of the frangipane.

Dust with icing sugar and serve with ice cream, if you like.

Sweet fondues served at the end of a meal make an easy, friendly dessert. Any sweet biscuits or cookies are good for dipping, but churros – the delicious doughnuts the Spanish serve with hot chocolate – work exceptionally well.

Bitter chocolate fondue with churros

300 g/10½ oz. dark/bittersweet chocolate
125 ml/½ cup double/heavy cream
¼ teaspoon dried chilli/hot red pepper flakes (optional)
2 tablespoons orange liqueur such as Cointreau (optional)
finely grated zest and juice of 2 oranges

FOR THE CHURROS
120 g/1 stick butter
150 g/1 cup plus 2 tablespoons plain/all-purpose flour, twice sifted
a pinch of salt
3 eggs, beaten
75 g/6 tablespoons caster/granulated sugar
2 teaspoons ground cinnamon
vegetable oil, for frying

a strong piping/pastry bag fitted with a 1-cm/½-inch star nozzle

Serves 6

To make the churros, heat 250 ml/1 cup cold water and the butter in a saucepan over a low heat until the butter melts. Tip in the flour and salt and beat well with a wooden spoon until the mixture comes away from the pan edges. Cool for 5 minutes. Whisk in the eggs, a little at a time, using electric beaters, until you have a smooth batter. Spoon into the piping bag.

Pour vegetable oil into a heavy-based saucepan to a depth of 5 cm/2 inches and heat until it reaches 180°C/350°F. Carefully pipe 12-cm/5-inch lengths of the dough straight into the hot oil, using scissors to cut the dough. Fry three churros at a time for 2–3 minutes until crisp and golden, turning halfway through using metal tongs. Remove with a slotted spoon and drain on paper towels.

Combine the sugar and cinnamon on a plate and roll the churros in the mixture until coated.

To prepare the fondue, put the chocolate into the top of a double boiler, add the cream, chilli flakes, liqueur, if using, and orange zest and juice. Heat over simmering water and stir until the sauce is melted and smooth. Transfer to a warmed fondue pot set over its tabletop burner. Serve with the churros for dipping.

Rum baba, a brioche-like dessert soaked in rum, is a French classic. Here the little buns are cooked, and rather than a rum syrup being poured over whilst hot, these are cooled and served with a fragrant orange sauce, either to dip or to drizzle.

Baba buns with caramelized orange sauce

1½ teaspoons dried active yeast

60 ml/4 tablespoons warm milk

2 tablespoons caster/granulated sugar

300 g/2¼ cups plain/all-purpose flour

a pinch of salt

3 eggs, beaten

60 g/4 tablespoons unsalted butter, softened, plus extra for greasing

pomegranate seeds, to serve

FOR THE CARAMELIZED ORANGE SAUCE

8 small oranges

100 g/½ cup caster/granulated sugar

4 tablespoons golden syrup/light corn syrup

100 g/7 tablespoons unsalted butter

100 ml/scant ½ cup double/heavy cream

1 tablespoon orange flower water

8 x 150-ml/⅔-cup timbales, greased

Serves 8

Whisk the yeast into the warm milk along with the sugar and leave for 10 minutes until frothy. Sift the flour and salt into the bowl of a stand mixer, add the frothed yeast mixture and eggs and bring together to form a sticky dough. Knead on a low speed for 2–3 minutes until it is starting to look elastic, then gradually beat in the butter, a little at a time, until incorporated. The mixture is very wet, more like a sponge batter than a bread dough. Cover the bowl with cling film/plastic wrap and leave to rise for 1–1½ hours until doubled in size.

Using a spoon, scoop out the risen dough and divide amongst the timbales. Using wet hands, smooth the surface flat and press down a little to remove air bubbles. Cover with oiled cling film and leave to rise for a further 30 minutes until the dough reaches the top of the timbales.

Preheat the oven to 170°C (325°F) Gas 3.

Remove the cling film and transfer the timbales to the preheated oven. Cook for 20 minutes until well risen and lightly golden. Cool in the timbales for 5 minutes, then turn out and cool on a wire rack.

Meanwhile, make the sauce. Peel four of the oranges, holding them over a small saucepan to catch any juices. Set them aside. Squeeze the juice from the remaining four oranges into the pan – you need 250 ml/1 cup juice, so make it up with a little water if necessary. Add the sugar and golden syrup to the saucepan and heat, stirring, until the sugar dissolves. Bring to the boil and cook without stirring for 10 minutes, or until the sauce is thickened and starting to turn a slightly darker colour. Carefully stir in the butter until melted and then the cream, and simmer for a further 3–4 minutes until thickened to the consistency of double/heavy cream. Stir in the orange flower water.

Cut the peeled oranges into thin slices and divide amongst serving plates with the babas and pomegranate seeds. Transfer the sauce to the tabletop burner. Cut the babas into slices or chunks and add to the serving plates.

There is something about the flavours of apple and cinnamon that just works so well in the colder months, and this delicious dessert is no exception.

Apple crêpes

140 g/1 cup plain/all-purpose flour, sifted
1 egg, plus 1 egg yolk
2 tablespoons melted butter, cooled, plus extra for frying
15 g/1 heaped tablespoon caster/granulated sugar
a pinch of salt
1 teaspoon ground cinnamon
300 ml/1¼ cups milk
250 ml/1 cup double/heavy cream, whipped to stiff peaks, to serve
icing sugar/confectioners' sugar, to serve

FOR THE APPLE COMPOTE

6 eating apples, peeled, cored and cut into small pieces
60 g/½ cup sultanas/golden raisins
1 teaspoon ground cinnamon, plus extra for dusting
100 g/½ cup caster/granulated sugar

Makes 10

Begin by preparing the apple compote. Put all of the ingredients and 125ml/½ cup water in a saucepan or pot set over a medium heat and simmer for 15–20 minutes until the apple is soft. Set aside to cool.

To make the crêpe batter, put the flour, egg and egg yolk, melted butter, caster sugar, salt and cinnamon in a large mixing bowl. Whisking all the time, gradually add the milk until you have a smooth and runny batter. Cover and put the batter in the refrigerator to rest for 30 minutes.

When you are ready to serve, remove the batter from the refrigerator and stir gently. Put a little butter in a large frying pan/skillet set over a medium heat. Allow the butter to melt and coat the base of the pan, then ladle a small amount of the rested batter into the pan and quickly spread it out very thinly. You can do this either by tilting the pan, or, for best results, use a crêpe swizzle stick. Cook until the top of the pancake is set, then turn over carefully with a spatula and cook on the other side for a further 1–2 minutes until the crêpe is golden brown. Keep the crêpes warm while you cook the remaining batter.

Spoon the apple compote and a little whipped cream onto one half of each crêpe, then fold the crêpe in half and then half again. Dust with ground cinnamon and icing sugar and serve.

The classic pumpkin pie is the inspiration for these crêpes, which are the perfect autumnal/fall dessert, with hints of cinnamon, ginger and vanilla.

Pumpkin chiffon crêpes

140 g/1 cup plain/all-purpose flour, sifted
1 egg, plus 1 egg yolk
2 tablespoons melted butter, cooled, plus extra for frying
15 g/1 heaped tablespoon caster/granulated sugar
1 teaspoon pure vanilla extract/vanilla bean paste
2 tablespoons pumpkin purée
a pinch of salt
300 ml/1¼ cups milk
300 ml/1¼ cups double/heavy cream, whipped to stiff peaks,

FOR THE PUMPKIN FILLING
250 g/2¼ cups pumpkin purée
3 eggs, separated
170 g/generous ¾ cup caster/granulated sugar
250 ml/1 cup milk
a pinch of salt or vanilla salt
1 teaspoon ground ginger
a pinch of freshly grated nutmeg
2 teaspoons ground cinnamon
1 teaspoon pure vanilla extract or vanilla bean paste
2 tablespoons melted butter
10 g/3 teaspoons powdered gelatine
60 ml/¾ cup warm water

TO SERVE
70 g/¾ cup pecans, finely chopped, to serve

Makes 10

Begin by preparing the filling. Put the pumpkin purée in a heatproof bowl set over a pot of boiling water and cook for 10 minutes to remove some of the liquid. While still over the heat, whisk in the egg yolks, 90 g/scant ½ cup of the caster sugar and all of the milk until you have a smooth mixture. Cook for 5 minutes more, then add the salt, ginger, nutmeg, cinnamon, vanilla extract and melted butter. Cook until the mixture thickens. Remove from the heat and set aside.

In a separate bowl, whisk the gelatine into the warm water until it dissolves, then stir it into the pumpkin mixture. Cover and chill in the refrigerator until set, ideally overnight.

Once the pumpkin mixture has set, whisk the egg whites to stiff peaks and then whisk in the remaining caster sugar, a tablespoonful at a time, to make a stiff meringue. Beat the pumpkin mixture a little to loosen it then fold the meringue into the pumpkin mixture. Chill until you are ready to serve.

To make the crêpe batter, put the flour, egg and egg yolk, melted butter, caster sugar, vanilla extract, pumpkin purée and salt in a mixing bowl. Whisking all the time, gradually add the milk until you have a smooth and runny batter. Cover and put the batter in the refrigerator to rest for 30 minutes.

Put a little butter in a large frying pan/skillet set over a medium heat. Allow the butter to melt and coat the base of the pan, then ladle a small amount of the rested batter into the pan. Cook until the batter on top is set, then turn over very carefully with a spatula and cook on the other side for a further 1–2 minutes until golden brown. Keep the crêpes warm while you cook the remaining batter in the same way.

To serve, put the crêpes in small bowls to form a basket shape. Fill with a spoonful of the pumpkin mixture and some whipped cream. Sprinkle with chopped pecans and serve.

SWEET THINGS

Creamy, indulgent waffles with a hint of alcohol, these are perfect to make after a long, hard day when you need a treat to relax with. The simplicity of the creamy, boozy sauce, finished with a little clotted cream, is divine.

Baileys waffles

260 g/2 cups self-raising/self-rising flour, sifted
60 g/scant ⅓ cup caster/granulated sugar
80 ml/scant ⅓ cup Baileys or other cream liqueur
a pinch of salt
3 eggs, separated
300 ml/1¼ cups milk
60 g/4 tablespoons butter, melted
clotted cream, to serve

FOR THE SAUCE
100 ml/7 tablespoons Baileys or other cream liqueur
200 ml/¾ cup double/heavy cream
50 g/3½ tablespoons butter
a pinch of salt
50 g/¼ cup caster/granulated sugar

an electric or stove-top waffle iron

Makes 8

Begin by preparing the sauce. Put all of the ingredients in a saucepan or pot set over a medium heat and simmer until the sugar and butter melt and the sauce begins to thicken. Keep the pan on the heat but turn it down to low to keep the sauce warm until you are ready to serve.

To make the waffle batter, put the flour, sugar, Baileys, salt, egg yolks, milk and melted butter in a large mixing bowl. Whisk until you have a smooth batter. In a separate mixing bowl, whisk the egg whites to stiff peaks and then gently fold into the batter, a third, at a time.

Preheat the waffle iron and grease with a little butter.

Ladle a small amount of the batter into the preheated waffle iron and cook the waffles for 3–5 minutes until golden brown. Keep the waffles warm while you cook the remaining batter in the same way.

Serve the waffles with the warm Baileys sauce and a teaspoon of clotted cream per portion.

What to do with leftover slightly stale croissants? Make this spiced apple and croissant bake, of course! This boozy, spiced pudding is rich and indulgent, ideal if you are looking for something a bit different from a basic apple pie and you have some croissants to use up. Serve with whipped cream or, for a true winter warmer, opt for lashings of custard.

Spiced apple & croissant bake with Calvados

500 ml/2 cups whole milk
500 ml/2 cups double/heavy cream
1 vanilla pod/bean, split
1 cinnamon stick
3 star anise
2 tablespoons Calvados
3 eggs, plus 3 egg yolks
200 g/1 cup caster/granulated sugar
2 croissants, slightly stale
30 g/2 tablespoons unsalted butter, melted
2 Braeburn apples or similar sweet yet tart eating apples
2 tablespoons semi-dried chopped apples
whipped cream or custard, to serve (optional)

Serves 4–6

Preheat the oven to 200°C (400°F) Gas 6 and grease a large pie dish or baking pan.

Put the milk, cream, vanilla, cinnamon, star anise and Calvados in a saucepan over a medium heat and bring just to the boil.

Meanwhile, put the eggs, egg yolks and sugar in a stand mixer or use a hand-held electric whisk to beat together until pale and fluffy. Slowly pour the boiled cream into the egg mixture, while whisking vigorously, until evenly incorporated.

Pass the mixture through a fine sieve/strainer and discard the vanilla pod, cinnamon stick and star anise.

Cut the croissants in half horizontally and brush the melted butter over them. Arrange them in the prepared dish.

Halve, core and roughly chop the fresh apples. Scatter these and the semi-dried apples over the croissants in the pan, then pour the custard in over the top. Using a spatula, press down the croissants so that they soak up some of the custard mixture.

Bake in the preheated oven for 25 minutes. The custard should still be a little runny in the middle. Serve with whipped cream or custard, if desired.

Cider, apples and butter with a hint of tangerine – what could be better? Grating the cooking apples makes a softer filling, which really melts in the mouth and is so easy to prepare. Dessert apples don't work as well – they are too sharp and won't collapse to a creaminess as tarter cooking apples (Bramleys) do. Serve with custard or cream.

Apple & buttered cider double-crust pie

1 sheet of ready-rolled shortcrust pastry
2 large cooking apples, peeled, cored and roughly grated
finely grated zest and freshly squeezed juice of 1 tangerine, or similar
75 g/5 tablespoons golden caster/natural cane sugar, plus 2 tablespoons for dredging
75 g/5 tablespoons butter, melted
2 tablespoons apple cider, apple brandy or Calvados
1 egg, beaten
whipped cream or custard, to serve (optional)

a 20-cm/8-inch (inside measurement) pie plate with a 2.5-cm/1-inch rim
a pie funnel
blossom pastry cutters (optional)

Serves 4

Preheat the oven to 200°C (400°F) Gas 6 and set a heavy baking sheet on the middle shelf.

Unroll the pastry on a lightly floured surface and cut it in half. Use half to line the pie plate, trim the edge and set a pie funnel in the middle.

Put the grated apple in a mixing bowl and add the tangerine zest and juice, sugar, 50 g/4 tablespoons of the melted butter (keep the remainder warm), the cider or brandy and the beaten egg. Mix well and spoon into the lined pie plate, levelling the surface.

From the remaining pastry, cut out a round slightly larger than the pie plate for the pie lid. Set aside. Cut out a long strip of pastry about 2.5 cm/1 inch wide and use it to line the rim of the dish, then brush with water. Make a hole in the middle of the pie lid and drape it over the pie plate, making sure that the hole drops over the pie funnel. Trim off the excess pastry and knock up the edges. If desired, use pastry cutters to cut shapes from any excess pastry and use them to decorate the top of the pie.

Set the pie on the baking sheet in the preheated oven and bake for 15 minutes. Reduce the temperature to 190°C (375°F) Gas 5 and bake for a further 15 minutes to set the pastry. Remove from the oven and brush with the remaining melted butter, dredge with the 2 tablespoons of sugar and return to the oven for a further 10–15 minutes until golden brown and crusty – watch closely as it may brown quickly.

Serve with cream or custard, as desired.

HOT DRINKS

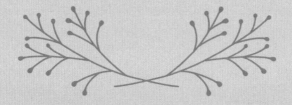

This is a strong coffee with a rich sweetness from the gooey caramel topping. You can vary this recipe by substituting the vanilla syrup with other flavours that you also enjoy. Gingerbread syrup works particularly well during the holiday season.

Caramel macchiato

2 tablespoons caramel sauce
1 tablespoon vanilla syrup
1–2 shots (30–60 ml/1–2 oz.) freshly brewed espresso coffee
250 ml/1 cup milk of your choice

piping/pastry bag, squeezy bottle or sundae spoon
milk steamer attachment or handheld electric milk frother

Serves 1

Prepare a heatproof glass by drizzling half of the caramel sauce in spiral patterns inside the glass. You can do this with a piping bag or by putting the sauce in a squeezy bottle and using it to make distinct lines. Alternatively, you can simply swirl in the sauce using a long-handled spoon.

Pour the vanilla syrup into the bottom of the prepared glass and pour in the hot coffee. Steam or froth the milk until hot and there is a thin layer of foam on top, and then pour over the coffee. Drizzle the remaining caramel sauce on top of the foam in a 'zig zag' pattern and serve at once.

Vanilla latte is a classic and you can buy good-quality vanilla syrups in supermarkets and online. Served with vanilla wafer rolls, this makes a lovely treat at any time during winter, but especially over the festive period.

Vanilla latte

1–2 tablespoon vanilla syrup, to taste
1–2 shots (30–60 ml/1–2 oz.)
   freshly brewed espresso coffee
250 ml/1 cup milk of your choice
a little vanilla bean powder, to sprinkle
vanilla wafer rolls, to serve (optional)

*milk steamer attachment or
   handheld electric milk frother*

Serves 1

Pour the vanilla syrup into the bottom of a cup or heatproof glass and pour in the hot coffee. Steam or froth the milk until very hot with a light layer of foam on top and then pour on top of the coffee. Serve at once with vanilla wafer rolls on the side, if liked.

Who doesn't love a good cinnamon bun? The smell when you take them out of the oven warm is utterly delicious. This coffee is made with a syrup similar to the sticky cinnamon bun filling and will brighten up any winter morning.

Cinnamon bun latte

100 ml/scant ½ cup double/
  heavy cream
1–2 shots (30—60 ml/1–2 oz.)
  freshly brewed espresso coffee
300 ml/1¼ cups milk of your choice
ground sweet cinnamon, to dust

FOR THE CINNAMON BUN SYRUP
1 tablespoon dark soft brown sugar
½ teaspoon ground sweet cinnamon
2 teaspoon butter

*milk steamer attachment or
  handheld electric milk frother*

Serves 1

Make the cinnamon bun syrup as it needs to cool before being whipped into the cream. Heat the brown sugar, cinnamon and butter with 1 tablespoon water in a saucepan over a gentle heat until you have a smooth thin syrup and the sugar has all dissolved. Set aside to cool.

When you are ready to serve your coffee, whip the cream with a third of the syrup until it forms soft peaks. Pour another third of the syrup into a cup or heatproof glass and pour over the hot coffee. Stir to incorporate the syrup into the coffee.

Steam or froth the milk until hot and foamy and pour over the coffee. Top with the whipped cinnamon bun cream, dust with a little cinnamon, drizzle over the remaining third of the syrup and serve at once.

For those of you who have not been fortunate enough to experience it, a 'fluffernutter' is a sandwich with layers of peanut butter and jarred marshmallow fluff. It is not for the faint-hearted as it is so very sweet, but an amazing twist on the classic peanut butter and jelly sandwich. This indulgent latte combines the peanut and marshmallow elements with a caffeine hit for the perfect sugary pick-me-up on a chilly winter day.

Fluffernutter latte

marshmallow fluff, to taste
2 tablespoons honey roasted peanuts, finely chopped
1 tablespoon smooth peanut butter
200 ml/scant 1 cup milk
1–2 shots (30—60 ml/1–2 oz.) freshly brewed espresso coffee

chefs' blow torch

a handheld electric milk frother or balloon whisk

Serves 1

First prepare a heatproof glass by dipping the top of it in a little marshmallow fluff and then press approximately half of the finely chopped peanuts into the fluff to decorate the rim. Set aside.

For the peanut milk, place the peanut butter in a saucepan with the milk and stir until the peanut butter melts into the milk. Froth the milk with a handheld electric frother or whisk until very foamy and the peanut butter and milk have blended together.

Pour the hot coffee into the prepared glass and top with the frothy peanut milk. Add a large spoonful of marshmallow fluff to the drink, then toast it with a chefs' blow torch to caramelize the marshmallow.

Sprinkle with the remaining chopped peanuts and serve at once.

This coffee is a coconut lover's dream, made with a sweet coconut syrup that flavours both the coffee and the creamy topping. Topped with toasted coconut and made with coconut milk, this drink is coconut-tastic! If you want to make this drink suitable for anyone with a dairy intolerance, just omit the cream topping.

Toasted coconut latte

1 tablespoon soft shredded coconut
100 ml/⅓ cup plus 1 tablespoon double/heavy cream (optional)
2–4 shots (60–120 ml/2–4 oz.) freshly brewed espresso coffee
500 ml/2 cups unsweetened coconut milk

FOR THE COCONUT SYRUP
20 g/1 tablespoon plus 2 teaspoons caster/granulated sugar
50 g/scant ¼ cup coconut cream

a handheld electric milk frother or balloon whisk

Serves 2

Make the coconut syrup first as it needs to cool before being whipped into the cream. Heat the sugar and coconut cream in a saucepan over a gentle heat until the sugar has dissolved, and you have a smooth thin syrup. Leave to cool.

Place the shredded coconut in a dry frying pan/skillet and toast until it starts to turn golden brown, stirring all the time as it can burn quickly. Once golden brown, remove from the pan and set aside until needed.

Place a spoonful of the cooled coconut syrup in two cups or heatproof glasses.

Whip the cream to soft peaks with the remainder of the coconut syrup.

Pour the hot coffee into the cups. Heat the coconut milk in a saucepan and use a handheld electric milk frother or whisk to whisk until foamy. Pour the coconut milk into each drink, top with a spoonful of coconut cream and sprinkle with the toasted coconut. Serve at once.

Every festive season there is always a Terry's chocolate orange from Santa, so this drink will instantly transport you to Christmas day mornings. If you cannot find a Terry's Chocolate Orange, you can easily substitute any plain/semisweet orange-flavoured chocolate bar.

Terry's chocolate orange hot chocolate

250 ml/1 cup milk of your choice
50 g/2 oz. Terry's chocolate orange, plus extra 'segments' to serve
whipped cream, to serve (canned is fine)
finely grated orange zest, to serve

a handheld electric milk frother or balloon whisk

Serves 1

Place the milk in a saucepan with the chocolate orange and simmer until melted, stirring all the time. Once the milk is hot, remove from the heat and froth with a handheld electric milk frother or whisk until all the chocolate is blended with the milk and the hot chocolate is very frothy.

Pour into a cup or heatproof glass and top with the whipped cream. Sprinkle over a little orange zest and decorate with 'segments' of chocolate orange. Serve at once.

This is a delicious hot chocolate drink with a grown-up kick. It is indulgent and warming with a splash of cherry brandy and a cute little maraschino cherry stick, which adds a touch of festive reindeer-nose red to the presentation! Serve with whipped cream on the side.

Cherry brandy hot chocolate

6 maraschino cherries
100 g/3½ oz. dark/bittersweet chocolate, chopped
1 tablespoon icing/confectioners' sugar
250 ml/1 cup milk of your choice
250 ml/1 cup double/heavy cream
5 tablespoons cherry brandy
2 tablespoons canned red or black cherry pie filling
whipped cream, to serve (optional)

Serves 2

Thread the cherries onto wooden skewers and set aside.

Place the chopped chocolate in a saucepan with the sugar, milk and double/heavy cream. Simmer over a low heat until the chocolate has melted, whisking all the time. Remove from the heat and add the cherry brandy.

Place a tablespoonful of cherry pie filling into the bottom of two heatproof glasses or cups, then carefully pour in the hot chocolate milk.

Place a cherry skewer in each glass. Serve at once with a small bowl of whipped cream on the side, if liked, ready to spoon into the drink. Have sundae spoons ready to enjoy the warm cherry pie filling at the bottom of the glass.

This is proper grown-up hot chocolate – manly hot chocolate if you will! Laced with bourbon whiskey and maple syrup it warms you to the core. It's a great drink for adults to take out in a flask for cold winter walks, but is also really special served at home in a praline-decorated cup.

Maple-pecan bourbon hot chocolate

100 g/3½ oz. milk chocolate, chopped
250 ml/1 cup double/heavy cream
250 ml/1 cup milk of your choice
100 ml/scant ½ cup maple syrup
1 teaspoon vanilla bean paste or pure vanilla extract
100 ml/scant ½ cup bourbon whiskey

FOR THE PECAN PRALINE
50 g/¼ cup caster/superfine sugar
3 tablespoons pecan halves

Serves 2

Make the pecan praline first. Heat the sugar in a saucepan until it melts, swirling the pan constantly. Do not stir with a spoon. Watch it carefully as it can burn very easily. Once the sugar is a golden caramel colour, spread the pecans out on a silicone mat or greased baking sheet, and then pour over the caramel. Leave to cool, then blitz to fine crumbs in a blender. Place the praline powder on a plate.

Next prepare two cups or heatproof glasses. Place the chopped chocolate in a heatproof bowl set over a pan of simmering water until melted — do not let the base of the bowl touch the surface of the water. Carefully dip the rim of each glass or cup into the melted chocolate, then roll the rim of each chocolate-rimmed glass in the praline powder. Set aside until ready to serve.

Spoon the remaining melted chocolate into a saucepan and add the cream, milk, maple syrup, vanilla and bourbon. Simmer over a low heat until combined, whisking all the time.

Pour the hot chocolate into the prepared glasses, taking care not to pour it over the decorated rims. Serve at once.

Brownies and hot chocolate are the perfect pair for a winter evening, and this hot chocolate is rich with all the flavours of a brownie – with cocoa and brown sugar. The drink is finished off with whipped marshmallow cream, grated chocolate and brownie pieces. This is probably the most indulgent drink in this book – enjoy!

Chocolate brownie mega hot chocolate

50 ml/3½ tablespoons double/heavy cream
1 tablespoon golden/light corn syrup
1 tablespoon cocoa powder
1 tablespoon brown sugar
½ teaspoon pure vanilla extract or vanilla bean paste
50 g/2 oz. dark/bittersweet chocolate, chopped
1 tablespoon melted butter
400 ml/1¾ cups milk of your choice
100 ml/3⅓ oz. double/heavy cream
2 tablespoons marshmallow fluff
1 teaspoon finely grated dark/bittersweet chocolate
1 chocolate brownie, cut into small pieces
mini marshmallows, to serve

a handheld electric milk frother or balloon whisk

Serves 2

In a saucepan, heat the cream with the syrup, cocoa powder, brown sugar and vanilla. Once the sugar has dissolved, add the chopped chocolate and butter and simmer until the chocolate is melted, stirring constantly. Add the milk and stir until the chocolate sauce is incorporated into the milk. Froth with a handheld electric milk frother or whisk until the chocolate milk is foamy.

In a bowl, whisk together the cream and marshmallow fluff until the mixture holds soft peaks. Pour the hot chocolate into two cups or heatproof glasses and top with the marshmallow cream, grated chocolate, a few small brownie pieces and some mini marshmallows. Serve at once.

Index

A

apples: apple & buttered cider double-crust pie 136
  apple-cranberry sauce 54
  apple crêpes 128
  spiced apple & croissant bake 135
apricot frangipane puddings 123
aubergines/eggplants: jacket stuffed with aubergine, harissa, crème fraiche & toasted pine nuts 62

B

baba buns with caramelized orange sauce 127
bacon: bacon, Brie & cranberry jackets 65
  beer & bacon pancakes 76
  goulash soup 19
  jacket with haggis & whisky sauce 70
  lentil & bacon soup 24
  weekend quesadillas 58
Baileys waffles 132
beef: goulash soup 19
  lasagne layered baked potato 61
  lasagne soup 15
  Philly cheesesteak sandwich 57
  truffled mash cottage pie 104
beer: ale, caramelized onion & thyme soup 20
  beer & bacon pancakes 76
biscuits see cookies & biscuits
bourbon: maple-pecan bourbon hot chocolate 154
bread: Brie & apple-cranberry toastie 54
  croute au fromage nature 41
  kimchi & Monterey Jack toastie 53
  Philly cheesesteak sandwich 57

broccoli: 'nduja, broccoli, black olive and egg pizza 87
  oven-baked broccoli & blue cheese gnocchi 96
brownies, chocolate 119
  chocolate brownie mega hot chocolate 157
butternut squash & chicory pasta bake 100

C

Calvados, spiced apple & croissant bake with 135
caramel macchiato 141
Caribbean sweet potato & coconut soup 27
cauliflower & leek gratin 46
cheese: ale, caramelized onion & thyme soup 20
  bacon, Brie & cranberry jackets 65
  blue cheese fondue with potato fries 38
  Brie & apple-cranberry toastie 54
  burrata, potato, sage & red onion marmellata pizza pie 88
  cauliflower & leek gratin 46
  cider fondue with pretzels 33
  classic fondue 45
  croute au fromage nature 41
  fish pie jacket 69
  fonduta 34
  French onion soup 16
  kimchi & Monterey Jack toastie 53
  lasagne layered baked potato 61
  lasagne soup 15
  mac 'n' cheese 95
  mushroom, blue cheese & walnut quiche 84
  mushroom, tarragon & Taleggio pasta bake 103
  oven-baked broccoli & blue cheese gnocchi 96
  pancetta, Gorgonzola & tomato mac 'n' cheese 99

Philly cheesesteak sandwich 57
  potato cheese pie 107
  Raclette over roasted potatoes 42
  Spanish cheese fondue with romesco 37
  weekend quesadillas 58
  Welsh rarebit waffles 49
cherry brandy hot chocolate 153
chicken: chicken & leek pot pie jackets 66
  cream of chicken soup 12
chicory: butternut squash & chicory pasta bake 100
chocolate: bitter chocolate fondue with churros 124
  chocolate brownies 119
  chocolate chip cookies 111, 115
  chocolate orange pillows 116
  hot chocolates 150–7
chorizo & black olive sausage rolls 80
churros 124
cider: apple & buttered cider double-crust pie 136
  cider fondue with pretzels 33
cinnamon: cinnamon & salted butter biscuits 112
  cinnamon bun latte 145
coconut milk: Caribbean sweet potato & coconut soup 27
  toasted coconut latte 149
coffee: caramel macchiato 141
  fluffernutter latte 146
  toasted coconut latte 149
  vanilla latte 142
compote, apple 128
cookies & biscuits:
  chocolate chip cookies 111, 115
  chocolate orange pillows 116
  cinnamon & salted butter biscuits 112
corned beef & sweet potato pasties 83

cottage pie, truffled mash 104
cranberry sauce: apple-cranberry sauce 54
  bacon, Brie & cranberry jackets 65
cream of chicken soup 12
creamy leek & potato soup 23
crêpes & pancakes: apple crêpes 128
  beer & bacon pancakes, 76
  pumpkin chiffon crêpes 131
croissants: spiced apple & croissant bake with Calvados 135
croute au fromage nature 41

D E

drinks 138–57
eggs: baked eggs 75
  'nduja, broccoli, black olive and egg pizza 87
  weekend quesadillas 58

F G

filo/phyllo pastry: individual pear strudels 120
fish pie jacket 69
fluffernutter latte 146
fondues: bitter chocolate fondue 124
  blue cheese fondue 38
  cider fondue 33
  classic fondue 45
  fonduta 34
  Spanish cheese fondue 37
frangipane puddings, apricot 123
French onion soup 16
fries, potato 38
gnocchi, oven-baked broccoli & blue cheese 96
goulash soup 19
gratin, cauliflower & leek 46
greens, Puy lentil & bacon soup with 24

158 INDEX

H J

haggis: jacket with haggis & whisky sauce 70
ham: creamy leek & potato soup 23
croute au fromage nature 41
hot chocolate 150–7
jacket potatoes: bacon, Brie & cranberry jackets 65
  chicken & leek pot pie jackets 66
  fish pie jacket 69
  jacket stuffed with aubergine, harissa, crème fraiche & toasted pine nuts 62
  jacket with haggis & whisky sauce 70
  lasagne layered baked potato 61

K L

kimchi & Monterey Jack toastie 53
lasagne: lasagne layered baked potato 61
  lasagne soup 15
lattes 142–9
leeks: cauliflower & leek gratin 46
  chicken & leek pot pie jackets 66
  creamy leek & potato soup 23
lentils: Puy lentil & bacon soup 24
  spiced lentil soup 11

M

mac 'n' cheese 95
  pancetta, Gorgonzola & tomato mac 'n' cheese 99
macchiato, caramel 141
marmellata, red onion 88
Marmite, tofu noodles with mushrooms & 92
mushrooms: creamy paprika mushrooms 91
  mushroom, blue cheese & walnut quiche 84
  mushroom, tarragon & Taleggio pasta bake 103
tofu noodles with mushrooms & Marmite 92

N O

'nduja: broccoli, black olive and egg pizza 87
noodles: tofu noodles with mushrooms & Marmite 92
  Vietnamese vegetable pho 28
olives: chorizo & black olive sausage rolls 80
  'nduja, broccoli, black olive and egg pizza 87
onions: ale, caramelized onion & thyme soup 20
  French onion soup 16
  Philly cheesesteak sandwich 57
  pickled red onion rings 38
  red onion marmellata 88
orange sauce, caramelized 127

P

pancetta, Gorgonzola & tomato mac 'n' cheese 99
pasta: butternut squash & chicory pasta bake 100
  lasagne soup 15
  mac 'n' cheese 95
  mushroom, tarragon & Taleggio pasta bake 103
  pancetta, Gorgonzola & tomato mac 'n' cheese 99
pasties, corned beef & sweet potato 83
pastrami: croute au fromage nature 41
pear strudels 120
pecans: maple-pecan bourbon hot chocolate 154
peppers: goulash soup with sour cream 19
  romesco sauce 37
Philly cheesesteak sandwich 57
pho, Vietnamese vegetable 28
pickled red onion rings 38

pies: apple & buttered cider double-crust pie 136
  potato cheese pie 107
pine nuts, jacket stuffed with aubergine, harissa, crème fraiche & toasted 62
pizza: burrata, potato, sage & red onion marmellata pizza pie 88
  'nduja, broccoli, black olive and egg pizza 87
potatoes: bacon, Brie & cranberry jackets 65
  burrata, potato, sage & red onion marmellata pizza pie 88
  chicken & leek pot pie jackets 66
  creamy leek & potato soup 23
  fish pie jacket 69
  jacket stuffed with aubergine, harissa, crème fraiche & toasted pine nuts 62
  jacket with haggis & whisky sauce 70
  lasagne layered baked potato 61
  potato cheese pie 107
  potato fries 38
  Raclette over roasted potatoes 42
  truffled mash cottage pie 104
pretzels 33
puff pastry: chicken & leek pot pie jackets 66
pumpkin chiffon crêpes 131

Q R

quesadillas, weekend 58
quiche, mushroom, blue cheese & walnut 84
Raclette over roasted potatoes 42
romesco, Spanish cheese fondue with 37
rye cookies, chocolate chip 111

S

sandwiches, Philly cheesesteak 57
sausages: chorizo & black olive sausage rolls 80
  simple sausage lattice slice 79
soups 8–29
Spanish cheese fondue with romesco 37
spiced apple & croissant bake 135
spiced lentil soup 11
squash: butternut squash & chicory pasta bake 100
strudel, individual pear 120
sweet potatoes: Caribbean sweet potato & coconut soup 27
  corned beef & sweet potato pasties 83

T

Terry's chocolate orange hot chocolate 150
toasted coconut latte 149
toasties: Brie & apple-cranberry toastie 54
  kimchi & Monterey Jack toastie 53
tofu noodles with mushrooms & Marmite 92
tomatoes: pancetta, Gorgonzola & tomato mac 'n' cheese 99
  Welsh rarebit waffles 49
tortilla wraps: weekend quesadillas 58
truffled mash cottage pie 104

V W

vanilla latte 142
Vietnamese vegetable pho 28
waffles: Baileys waffles 132
  Welsh rarebit waffles 49
walnuts: mushroom, blue cheese & walnut quiche 84
weekend quesadillas 58
Welsh rarebit waffles 49
whisky sauce 70

INDEX **159**

Credits

RECIPE CREDITS

MAXINE CLARK
Apple & Buttered Cider Double Crust Pie
Burrata, Potato, Sage & Red Onion Marmelatta Pizza Pie
Chorizo & Black Olive Sausage Rolls
Corned Beef & Sweet Potato Pasties
'Nduja, Broccoli, Black Olive & Egg Pizza
Simple Sausage Lattice Slice

MEGAN DAVIES
Baked Eggs
Butternut Squash & Chicory Pasta Bake
Cauliflower & Leek Gratin
Cinnamon & Salted Butter Biscuits
Tofu Noodles with Mushrooms & Marmite
Weekend Quesadillas

LIZ FRANKLIN
Chocolate Orange Pillows
Classic Choc Chip Cookies

DUNJA GULIN
Individual Pear Strudels

TORI HASCHKA
Apricot Frangipane Puddings

CAROL HILKER
Chocolate Brownies

LIZZIE KAMENETZKY
French Onion Soup with Comté toasts
Goulash Soup

KATHY KORDALIS
Chocolate Chip Rye Cookies

JENNY LINFORD
Mushroom, Blue Cheese & Walnut Quiche
Potato & Cheese Pie
Truffled Mash Cottage Pie

THEO A. MICHAELS
Classic Fondue
Oven-baked Broccoli & Blue Cheese Gnocchi

HANNAH MILES
Apple crêpes
Bacon, Brie & Cranberry Jackets
Bailey's Waffles
Beer & Bacon Pancakes
Caramel Macchiato
Caribbean Sweet Potato & Coconut Soup
Cherry Brandy Hot Chocolate
Chicken & Leek Pot Pie Jackets
Chocolate Brownie Mega Hot Chocolate
Cinnamon Bun Latte
Cream of Chicken Soup
Creamy Paprika Mushrooms
Fish Pie Jacket
Fluffernutter Latte
Jacket with Haggis & Whisky Sauce
Jacket Stuffed with Aubergine with crème fraiche & toasted pine nuts
Lasagne Layered Baked Potato
Lasagna Soup
Maple Pecan Bourbon Hot Chocolate
Pumpkin Chiffon Crêpes
Spiced Lentil Soup
Terry's Chocolate Orange Hot Chocolate
Toasted Coconut Latte
Vanilla Latte
Vietnamese Vegetable Pho
Welsh Rarebit Waffles

LOUISE PICKFORD
Baba Buns with Caramelized Orange Sauce
Bitter Chocolate Fondue with Churros
Blue Cheese Fondue with Potato Fries
Cider Fondue with pretzels
Croute au Fromage Nature
Fonduta
Raclette over Roasted Potatoes
Spanish Cheese Fondue with romesco

WILL TORRENT
Spiced Apple & Croissant Bake with Calvados

LAURA WASHBURN HUTTON
Brie & Apple-Cranberry Toastie
Classic Mac 'n' Cheese
Kimchi & Monterey Jack Toastie
Mushroom, Tarragon & Taleggio Pasta Bake
Pancetta, Gorgonzola & Tomato Mac 'n' Cheese
Philly Cheesesteak Sandwich

BELINDA WILLIAMS
Ale, Caramelized Onion & Thyme Soup
Creamy Leek & Potato Soup with ham hock
Puy Lentil & Bacon Soup with seasonal greens

PHOTOGRAPHY CREDITS

ED ANDERSON
Page 27.

TIM ATKINS
Page 80.

PETER CASSIDY
Pages 118, 142.

JONATHON GREGSON
Page 134.

MOWIE KAY
Pages 44, 86, 89, 97, 110, 135.

ADRIAN LAWRENCE
Page 141.

ALEX LUCK
Pages 13, 14, 26, 138, 140, 143, 144, 147, 148, 151, 156.

STEVE PAINTER
Pages 2, 10, 21, 22, 25, 29, 30, 48, 52, 55, 56, 60, 62, 63, 64, 67, 68, 71, 77, 78, 81, 82, 90, 94, 98, 102, 120, 129, 130, 133, 137, 152, 153, 155.

RITA PLATTS
Pages 47, 59, 74, 93, 101, 113.

NASSIMA ROTHACKER
Pages 17, 18, 19.

IAN WALLACE
Pages 1, 4, 8, 11, 12, 32, 35, 36, 39, 40, 43, 95, 107, 108, 124, 125, 126.

ISOBEL WELD
Page 122.

KATE WHITTAKER
Pages 3, 7, 23, 50, 84, 91, 114, 117, 149.

CLARE WINFIELD
Pages 5, 53, 58, 65, 69, 72, 76, 85, 87, 105, 106, 111, 119, 121.